SPEAKERS OF THE HOUSE

JUDITH BENTLEY
FOREWORD BY THOMAS S. FOLEY

DEMOCRACY IN ACTION
FRANKLIN WATTS
NEW YORK/CHICAGO/LONDON/TORONTO/SYDNEY

328.73
Ben

Photographs copyright ©: Wide World Photos: pp. 22, 100, 134, 143; Reuters/Bettmann Newsphotos: p. 26; New York Public Library, Picture Collection: pp. 37, 86, 98; The Bettmann Archive: pp. 49, 51; North Wind Picture Archives, Alfred, Me.: pp. 53, 55, 63; The Library of Congress: pp. 78, 81; UPI/Bettmann Newsphotos: pp. 91, 106, 109, 121, 135; The Sam Rayburn Library, Bonham, Tex.: p. 95; Gamma-Liaison: pp. 124 (Penelope Breese), 127 (Dirck Halstead).

Library of Congress Cataloging-in-Publication Data

Bentley, Judith.
Speakers of the House / Judith Bentley.
p.   cm.
Includes bibliographical references and index.
ISBN 0-531-11156-3 (lib. bdg.)
1. United States. Congress. House—Speaker—History.   I. Title
II. Series: Democracy in action (Franklin Watts, inc.)
JK1411.B45   1994
328.73'0762—dc20   94-15073
CIP AC

Copyright © 1994 by Judith Bentley
All rights reserved
Printed in the United States of America
6 5 4 3 2 1

CONTENTS

FOREWORD
by Thomas S. Foley
9

INTRODUCTION
"POWER AND ORDER IN THE HOUSE"
16

1
TOM FOLEY AND THE DEFICIT
19

2
HENRY CLAY AND SLAVERY
32

3
THOMAS BRACKETT REED AND THE RULES
57

4
JOE CANNON AND PROGRESS
73

5
SAM RAYBURN AND CIVIL RIGHTS
93

6
TIP O'NEILL AND THE CONTRAS
119

EPILOGUE:
"SEEKING THE MODERATE MIDDLE"
137

SOURCE NOTES
145

BIBLIOGRAPHY
153

INDEX
155

SPEAKERS OF THE HOUSE

FOREWORD

I have served in the United States House of Representatives for thirty years, and for the past five years I have had the honor of serving as the forty-ninth Speaker. Every Speaker has brought something different to the office, which has been a dynamic part of our democracy. In representative government, the House, under the leadership of the Speaker, reflects the will of the people, and the speakership is not only the strong central seat of authority, but the seat of change. The Speaker can be the singular voice of partisanship and power or the voice of consensus and reason.

As we approach the twenty-first century, our government is in transition. In fact, we are in a critical period in the history of American democracy. The world has undergone a transformation: The cold war has ended, new players now fill major roles on the world stage, and we are moving toward a global economy. Moreover, we have witnessed a period of astounding scientific and technological advancement, and the next century promises even greater breakthroughs. For example, we are on the threshold of a revolution in electronic communications, networking, and new developments in medical technology that continue to astound us every day. But in the next century, these achievements will not come easily; our future will greatly depend on how well we prepare for and meet the challenges that are before us today.

The 435 members of the House of Representatives are chosen by the American people to represent their interests in deciding the most critical issues of the day. Each member of Congress represents a different constituency with different needs and concerns, and thus each brings a unique perspective to the job. But they all share one common goal—to develop the most effective legislation possible for the good of the nation. This can only be done by working together toward a consensus, taking into consideration the diverse interests of Americans as well as the primary national interest, to preserve and protect the American community.

The House is faced with the task of reaching consensus on complex issues such as health care reform, welfare reform, and crime and violence in America, and it is the challenge of the Speaker to lead the effort. The post–cold war world, with all of its problems and potential, may not always accede to our individual desire to be right, but it requires that we act together because history demands it, and the American people deserve it. By virtue of circumstance and good fortune, we are at the threshold of great accomplishments, and we are determined not to let this opportunity pass.

Our founders predicted that history would test the ability of democratic institutions to accommodate change as America grew. They were right. Since then, America's role in the world has changed as events have tested our economic and political strength, as well as our resolve as a people and a government to preserve democracy, freedom, and justice. As Speaker during a transitional period in history, I have come to respect the words of Thomas Jefferson, who was most adamant about the responsibility of each generation to reconsider the means by which it is governed. Jefferson said, "I am certainly not an advocate for frequent and untried changes in laws and constitutions. I think moderate imperfections had better be borne with, because, when once known, we accommodate ourselves to them and find practical means of correcting their ill effects. But, I know also," he said, "that laws and institutions must go hand in hand with the progress of the human mind. As that becomes more developed, more enlightened, as new discoveries are made, new truths disclosed, and manners and opinions change with the change of circumstances, institutions must advance also, and keep pace with the times."

Jefferson knew that the challenge of each generation is to pursue a course of political reform that enhances the virtues of democracy. Our mandate in Congress, as representatives of the people, and the mandate of every Speaker as leader of the Congress, is to balance the spirit of Jefferson with the wisdom of James Madison—to welcome change that strengthens our form of government, reinforces the comparative advantages of the legislative and executive branches, and "works," as Madison said, "to refine and enlarge public views."

The single most important task of the Speaker of the House is to preserve and enhance Congress's ability to represent and to deliberate. In other words, it is for him, or her, to move the members of Congress, with their individual views and diverse constituencies, toward compromise and accommodation in order to enact responsible legislation that is in the best interest of every American. It was said in a recent study "Renewing Congress," by the American Enterprise Institute and the Brookings Institution, "where a consensus exists in the country, Congress should be structured to articulate, deliberate, and act upon that sentiment, enabling the voices of majorities to ring louder than the extremes. Where the public is divided on a crucial problem facing the country, Congress should work to form a consensus rather than hardening those differences and perpetuating policy deadlock."

As you read about the speakership, I hope that what becomes profoundly clear is that our system of government works. It is a grand experiment in freedom shaped, in part, by the stories of leadership in this book. But, while these stories represent but a small part of our history, they provide a glimpse at the courage, dedication, and sacrifice that have gone into the building of our great nation. The history of civilization is littered with tales of the scurrilous and the corrupt, of those who might abuse power or invoke privilege for something other than the common good. But there are many more examples of men and women who have dedicated their lives to the best traditions of public service and to the proliferation of hope and freedom in the world.

What the reader will learn from this book is essential to informed discussion about Congress and to public education about the House; in these pages are genuine insights into one of the most fundamental aspects of the House of Representatives, the speakership. The office I inherited from my predecessors is very different from what it was in the early years of our government, just as the institution of Congress is very different. I came to Congress in 1965 as a freshman reformer, and I learned how difficult it was to find support for new ideas when the leadership was reluctant to make more changes after the congressional reforms of 1945.

When I arrived in Congress there was a rigid power monopoly for a few senior members. Some of us thought that was wrong and should be changed. Eventually, through the Democratic Caucus, we sought a forum for junior members who wanted a greater role in the process. Through the Democratic Caucus we pressed for reforms that would open the process, and passed the Legislative Reorganization Act of 1970 and the Bolling-Hansen Committee Reforms of 1974. The changes we made were a sign of the times. They made every member more independent, and enhanced every member's participation in the legislative process which was reserved for the more senior members.

Along the way, the speakership has gone through many changes, but it has remained the most powerful position in Congress. In recent years the authority of the speakership has been strengthened. The most significant changes gave the Speaker control over the Rules Committee, and the power of multiple referral of bills to committees, enabling the Speaker to have control over the legislative process from beginning to end. The Speaker has also gained more influence over the budget process, the development of a budget resolution, and over negotiations of the final budget product. Therefore, when I was elected Speaker in 1989, I assumed an office that had more institutional power at its disposal than my immediate predecessors had. Yet the legislative process and the influence of individual members had been enhanced. Today, the Speaker's job is to use the power of the office to lead 435 members, representing 250 million diverse people, through debate and discussion, and ultimately to a consensus on legislation in the best interest of everyone.

The legislative process and the issues before us are now more complex than ever. In the new information age, instant input and public participation in what used to be private deliberations have opened the debate to public scrutiny. Too often the intensity of the debate and the conflicting convictions of individual members are viewed by the public as an indication of the failure of the system when, in fact, it is an essential part of the democratic process. But today members rightly expect that when they come to Congress they will begin immediately to act on their convictions and to represent the specific interest of the constituencies without any diminution of their rights to speak and express their opinions. While authority is still respected in the House, it is in a different context than the more uncritical acceptance of absolute power in the leadership that I found when I first came to Congress.

Today, the bright lights of public scrutiny shine on the process and emphasize every blemish. Unfortunately, the public debate of complex issues placed under the magnifying lens of the media has led to a pervasive misconception that government and Congress are unwilling and unable to act, when in fact the process is working as our founders intended. Public frustration sometimes runs high, because we are watching a deliberative government crafted by its founders to avoid extremes and prevent tyranny. It is a process designed for the purpose of debate, deliberation, and compromise. Such a process is necessarily ponderous and slow, but therein lies its virtue.

If Americans could observe the congressional process up close, traveling with members to committee hearings and meetings, and then to their districts and local town hall meetings, they would come away with an enormously enhanced understanding of how the House works. I believe they would also come away with a renewed faith in public service, a noble profession that attracts dedicated men and women who work hard for the preservation of our system of government and in the best interest of every American.

Most Americans will never be able to spend time in Congress to observe it firsthand, but by reading about it they can get a perspective on how different Speakers approached the job, how their minds worked, and how their personalities and characters played a part in their decision-making. *Speakers of the House* provides such a perspective, and will thus be an extremely valuable book for young readers who want to learn more about how our system works.

The lessons of history provide a window to the future, and there are important history lessons to be learned from reading this book. The reader will no doubt come

FOREWORD

away with a clear sense of who we are as a nation, a better understanding of what America stands for, and an acquaintance with some of the basic principles that have guided us throughout our nation's history. Because these principles will guide our successors as they have those who came before us, it is essential that young people grasp their meaning now. After all, in the next century it will be up to them alone to fulfill the promise of their generation.

In this volume, Judith Bentley's profiles of six Speakers from the nineteenth and twentieth centuries combine to form a dramatic historical account, not only of the speakership but of American democracy in action. The stories of Henry Clay, Thomas Brackett Reed, Joe Cannon, Sam Rayburn, and Tip O'Neill presented in this rich and readable book combine to form a portrait of leadership in a representative democracy, and offer valuable lessons for every American, for members of Congress, and even for Speakers. Each of these men, in his own way, made the speakership work, and I am proud to be among them.

Tom Foley, Speaker
United States House of Representatives
February 1994

INTRODUCTION
"POWER AND ORDER IN THE HOUSE"

If you tour the Capitol in Washington, D.C., on a pre-arranged visit, you may be invited to try out the Speaker's chair. The high-backed leather armchair sits all alone on a dais above the floor of the House of Representatives chamber. Some who try out the chair perch gingerly, their feet dangling. A few of the more daring swivel around. Almost all smile, for the experience conveys a brief sense of power, the authority the Speakers have when they gavel the House to order.

Certainly the architects and artists of the Capitol intended a grand effect, from the huge American flag hanging behind the Speaker's chair and the four black marble pillars framing it to the rich cream, gold, and crimson carpet of the semicircular floor. To the Speaker's right, ornate doors lead to the Speaker's lobby, where representatives congregate to talk about the concerns of the day.

If you sat in that chair or in the gallery on a typical legislative day, representatives from all fifty states—from California cities to New York suburbs, from Illinois farms to Texas ranches—would stand to be asked by the Speaker of the House, "To what purpose does the gentleman [or gentlewoman] rise?" When permission is granted "without objection," they speak on every issue even briefly troubling the nation: on a drought in California, trade with Japan, parental leave to care for sick children, gun control, the deficit, welfare reform, or funds for the Small Business Administration. Because of the Speaker's leadership of the House, where every national issue is debated, the position is regarded as the second most powerful in the land, after the presidency.

Were you to remain in the Speaker's chair, the sense of power and grandeur might seem fleeting. Gathered before you on a full legislative day would be 434 other representatives with 434 different opinions who would vote 434 different ways on every issue if they could, after giving 434 slightly different speeches on the subject. Your job as Speaker would be to see that they did debate and vote, in as civilized a manner as passion would allow.

Far more than merely presiding, however, the Speaker must pull diverse people and views together to reach at least a momentary consensus. Most of that work goes on out of the chair and off the floor, in the Speaker's lobby and offices, the hallways and conference rooms. Order comes from the chair; power is more diffuse.

Forty-nine different Speakers have sat in that chair and wielded power in the more than two hundred years since Congress first met in 1789. Six Speakers from different times demonstrate the power of the position and the way each Speaker uses it to influence legislation.

Henry Clay, for example, became Speaker in 1811, at the relatively young age of thirty-four. A nationalist from the frontier state of Kentucky, he tenaciously held the young nation together through its most divisive fight—over the expansion of slavery.

When Thomas Brackett Reed became Speaker in 1890, the westward movement had filled the country. Such geographic and economic expansion brought new divisions to the House debates, which Reed sought to bridge with the strength of his intellect and will.

After Reed, Joseph Cannon of Illinois presided so dictatorially from the chair that he was ousted by the forces of progress in his own Republican party.

Sam Rayburn dominated the House for seventeen years as Speaker in the 1940s, 1950s, and early 1960s, gradually moving himself and the country to a broader view on civil rights.

Tip O'Neill held off President Reagan's demands for military aid to the contras in Nicaragua for two years but finally could not withstand the intense lobbying of a popular, persistent president.

Thomas Foley assumed leadership for the 1990s and soon tackled a deficit that had been accumulating for decades of government spending and borrowing.

Let us begin in the present with the view from the Speaker's chair as he forges some agreement, however temporary, on the great issues of the day.

1

TOM FOLEY AND THE DEFICIT

"The speakership isn't a dictatorship."

At 8:00 P.M. on an October night in 1990, the weary Democratic leadership of the House of Representatives huddled in the Speaker's office. All day long, the majority leader, Richard Gephardt, had been counting votes. He was forty votes short. As the leaders gathered around the Speaker, Tom Foley, they debated the next step.

The issue was the federal deficit, estimated at $3 trillion: $3,000,000,000,000. The deficit for 1990 alone was likely to be $300 billion ($300,000,000,000), which would break the record for a one-year deficit. The interest on the debt was running almost $275 billion annually, making it the third largest government outlay after national defense and social security.

For months the leaders of Congress and the president had been trying to work a deal they could both support: a five-year plan to make a real stab at controlling the monster. When the "summiteers" finally reached a compromise and presented it to the House, the representatives were refusing to go along. Gephardt couldn't find forty more votes from Democrats or Republicans.

How had this impasse developed? Finding votes to raise taxes and cut spending is never easy. Ever since the Civil War, the United States government has been borrowing money to pay its bills. The debt reached $1 billion before World War I, then $25 billion by 1921. In one decade, from 1980 to 1990, the national debt owed by every single American man, woman, and child had more than tripled, from $3,989 to $12,409.

Government spending in five categories—federal unemployment insurance payments, Medicare, federal salaries, certain health and human services, and interest on the debt itself—was increasing at annual rates of 10 to 24 percent. Two of these categories—Medicare and interest—were increasing by $1 billion a month. More alarmingly, the government was borrowing money to pay the interest on money it had already borrowed. The debt was feeding itself.

Why is this a problem? The money is owed to thousands of people who buy U.S. Savings Bonds or who invest in Treasury bills. The debt is also owed to foreign governments who buy the bonds and securities the U.S. government issues to build highways, dams, nuclear weapons plants, and national parks. If any of the investors—big or little—lose faith in the government's ability to pay back the loans with interest, they will no longer lend the United States money.

Until the 1990s the government had done little to try to stop the binge. Even as the debt bulged in the 1980s, President Reagan proposed tax cuts, which Congress approved, thus decreasing revenue to the government. When the president asked for increases in military spending, the Democrats agreed but also protected such popular "safety net" programs as Social Security and Medicare. In addition to the huge military buildup, Congress approved a war on drugs, farm subsidies, money for housing, bridges, clean air, clean water, and veterans' benefits. Very few of these programs had actually been paid for.

In the 101st Congress the debt came to rest on the

tall frame and slightly hunched shoulders of Tom Foley. The sixty-one-year-old Democrat from Washington State had been in the House since the Lyndon Johnson landslide of 1964. Foley defeated a Republican in a Republican district that includes the city of Spokane near the Idaho border.

Foley came in as a liberal on issues but a moderate in style. Because of his thoughtful, open-minded approach, the members have twice voted him "the most respected man in the House." His skills in dealing with people earned him the label "Friendly Foley."[1]

Since the 1964 election his life has been committed to the legislative process. His wife, Heather, works full-time as his unpaid office manager and is known as the best staff person in the House. A faithful small Belgian shepherd, Alice, used to follow him around the labyrinthine corridors of the Capitol.

Although Foley seems unambitious beside his colleagues, over the years he worked his way up the leadership ladder. He was named majority whip, the third highest leadership position in the House, in 1981 by Speaker Thomas P. ("Tip") O'Neill. The whip's job is to round up party support and votes for pending legislation. In 1987, when O'Neill retired and James Wright of Texas became Speaker, Foley moved up to majority leader, the Speaker's deputy on the House floor.

Just two years later, Wright resigned after a House committee investigation. The committee charged that he had accepted gifts and avoided limits on outside income. Wright concluded he had been too partisan and aroused the anger of the opposition Republicans. The more mild-mannered Foley became Speaker.

Unlike his fiery predecessor, Foley is regarded as a cautious man and a coalition builder. A staff aide predicted Foley would lead with a velvet glove. "It's going to be more like high tea in Britain than a shoot-out at the O.K. Corral."[2]

Called "Friendly Foley" for his skills in dealing with people and building coalitions, Speaker Tom Foley must chart the middle ground when dealing with issues such as national health care, tax increases, military cutbacks, and environmental legislation.

Leading Congress is no small task. As the legislative branch of the federal government has grown in size and complexity, power is shared among a large number of people. In addition to the Speaker at the top, there are majority and minority leaders, majority and minority whips, deputy whips, committee chairs, and 265 subcommittee chairs. There are also less institutionalized groups, such as the party caucuses and interest caucuses: the Congressional Black Caucus, the Women's Caucus, the freshman caucus, and the Conservative Caucus.

Moreover, for a decade American voters had consistently elected a divided government, a Republican president and a Democratic Congress. Thus no one party was able to dominate. The president could suggest legislation, but Congress had to pass it. Congress could pass legislation, but the president had to sign it. While Wright was Speaker, President George Bush vetoed fifteen bills, and Congress was unable to override any of them with a two-thirds majority.

When Foley became Speaker, he set out to ease the acrimony that had developed between the Democrats and Republicans. "My overriding desire is to return the House to an atmosphere of collegiality, comity and mutual respect," Foley declared.[3]

His first opportunity came in the summer of 1989. Presiding in the chair, he called for a voice vote on an issue before the House. In the previous thirty-five years, no matter how many people shouted yes or no, the Democrats always won because the Speaker hearing the shouts was a Democrat. On this day there was a voice vote, and the few Democrats on the floor at the time shouted yes. The Republicans, present in much greater number, shouted no.

Foley ruled the noes had it.

The Democrats were so stunned they didn't know what to do. "Finally they got the word," recounts Representative Mickey Edwards, a Republican, "and one of them asked for a recorded vote and we had it. And at that point, every Republican on the floor rose spontaneously and gave Tom Foley a standing ovation."[4]

By this action, Foley demonstrated his great respect for the rules and institution of the House and for the process of legislating. He also conveyed his idea of the Speaker as a leader who must be fair to both parties, the majority and the minority. Once he had set a more cooperative tone, Foley began work on his second priority, "getting the House back to a national agenda."[5] At the top of that agenda was the deficit. Foley himself had no strong views on how to reduce the deficit, but he regarded it as the nation's most serious problem, which he was determined to tackle in his first full term.

The 101st Congress was not the first to try to deal with the deficit, but the temptation to spend money usually won. In a quest for self-discipline in 1985, the House had taken the drastic step of devising a fiscal straitjacket. The Gramm-Rudman-Hollings law was passed, mandating automatic reductions in spending if the House failed to devise a budget that would reduce the deficit. In the five years after that, however, the government had still found ways to avoid the reductions.

Fiscal restraint is decidedly unpopular in Congress and requires more than one person's or one party's support. Budget writing is also a complicated task. The Constitution gives the House the power to originate money and tax bills, but the budget must be approved by the Senate and signed by the president. The Democrats had a majority in the House and could pass any budget they could agree on, but they did not have enough votes to override a presidential veto. So a pattern of conferring between the executive branch and congressional leaders had been established. Congressional leaders would then present a package deal to Congress for approval with the expectation that it would not be vetoed. Following that pattern, Foley and House Democrats were prepared to work with everyone, at first: with the Republican minority in the House, with Republican president George Bush, with the president's staff, and with the Senate, where Democrats had a ten-vote margin.

In the spring of 1990, however, all of those people had trouble even talking about the deficit. President Bush had promised repeatedly in his 1988 campaign that he would not raise taxes—"Read my lips: no new taxes." The president's staff was worried that the deficit would propel the economy toward recession, but they didn't want to mention taxes either. Half of the members of the House were running for reelection that fall, and they certainly didn't want to talk about taxes. Some Democrats had been defeated by Republicans who claimed the Democrats were the "tax and spend party," so Democrats insisted they would not even whisper "taxes" this time around.

"There's not going to be a Democratic pounding on the door to raise taxes and a rejection by the president," Foley warned.[6]

Meanwhile, the deficit grew. At the rate it was increasing, Congress would be forced by its own Gramm-Rudman law to make 20 percent cuts, or $74 billion, beginning October 15. Twenty percent cuts, everyone agreed, would be too much. Early in May, President Bush took the initiative by calling for a budget summit between House and Senate leaders, the president, and his staff.

When they finally started talking, however, the discussions went nowhere for several weeks. No one wanted to mention the "T word" first, not Richard Darman, the budget director, not John Sununu, Bush's chief of staff, Nicholas Brady, secretary of the treasury, Lloyd Bentsen, chair of the Senate Finance Committee, Gephardt, or Foley. After many breakfast, lunch, and evening meetings at the White House, the president finally agreed that he would mention it first. To be exact, he agreed to

During the years of the Bush administration, Tom Foley's expertise in the art of compromise was put to the test when he presented a plan for spending cuts and tax increases that would reduce the budget deficit.

say that the size of the deficit required a package of items including "tax revenue increases."[7]

Once the magic words were uttered on June 16, the budget summit resumed but deadlocked again over who would put forth a specific proposal first. Such niggling, distrust, and genuine disagreement as to how to attack the deficit went on for five months.

There were no easy solutions. Cut military spending at a time when Bush had committed 250,000 troops to Saudi Arabia? Cut Medicare or Social Security for the elderly, who vote in a greater percentage than any other age group? Change the tax structure so soon after it had been reformed in 1984? Increase taxes for an electorate that had clearly voted against them?

Despite the distastefulness of any solution, on the last day of September, President Bush gathered the summiteers around him in the Rose Garden to announce an agreement. Taxes would be raised on gasoline, oil, yachts, liquor, and cigarettes. Spending on Medicare, which provides medical care to the elderly, would be cut. The plan would reduce the deficit by $500 billion over the next five years.

It was Tom Foley's job to present the plan to the House. Bush had promised to seek public support and round up Republican votes. With the help of Gephardt and Majority Whip William Gray, the Speaker would find Democratic votes.

For the task of bringing representatives together, Foley has great patience. His ears that cartoonists draw large are an accurate indication he will listen forever to all sides of an issue and hope that a consensus emerges. In fact, Speaker O'Neill used to chide him for seeing three sides to every issue. A colleague once asked Foley to give him three reasons for voting against a pending bill, which Foley did. The representative voted against the bill, and he was stunned when Foley voted for it. When he asked why, Foley said he could have given him three better reasons to vote for the bill but the man had not asked.[8]

Some of his fellow Democrats criticize Foley for being too conciliatory. They think he should define a Democratic agenda and pursue it. Foley disagrees. "A Speaker can be a catalyst, even to some extent, a source of direction," he says. "But it's like everything else in the Congress. . . . It's a collective effort. There is a degree to which you can sort of push, encourage, support, direct, but the speakership isn't a dictatorship."[9]

With the budget, Foley had worked for consensus between the executive and legislative branches, between the Republicans and Democrats. Contrary to his usual style, he was trying to sell the package to representatives. The sell wasn't working. Even when President Bush made a television speech attempting to rally public support, he aroused public opposition instead, especially to the increased gasoline taxes and cuts in Medicare. With telephone and mail messages pouring into congressional offices, representatives running for reelection were particularly reluctant to go along with the summit deal.

A riddle circulated among representatives who felt their opinions had not been heard during the summit: "What's the difference between Mouseketeers and Summiteers? Mouseketeers have ears."[10] Congress seemed to have ears only for the complaints coming from constituents.

Thursday, October 4, was a frantic round of vote seeking. In a closed-door Democratic caucus in the morning, the normally calm Foley gave "the most emotional speech of his career," asking for support for a plan he didn't much like but thought was necessary.[11] Bush wooed sixty Republicans over coffee and doughnuts at the White House. At lunch, Bush and Foley discussed strategy.

That evening the Democratic leaders gathered in Foley's office. Although Gephardt reported that they were forty votes short, there seemed to be no advantage in delaying longer. The Speaker decided to go ahead with the vote.

Much later that night, Foley stepped down from the Speaker's chair into the "well." The well is the position on the House floor in front of the dais. Members speak from two microphones there, but the Speaker rarely addresses the House. Foley felt the budget deal was important enough to require the cooperation of all members and his personal support.

"Mr. Speaker, I take the well seldom," he began. "I take it tonight late in the legislative day—late, perhaps, in the life of our country—to deal with a critical problem we have all ignored too long. Members of the Congress have ignored it, members of both parties have ignored it, Presidents have ignored it. . . .

"This budget resolution is the result of a much-decried summitry which is . . . the result of a divided Government in which there is a Republican President and a Congress led by majorities of the Democratic Party. The problem is not divided into a Republican problem and a Democratic problem; it is a problem that faces all of us. It faces the country and it affects every American. . . ."[12]

Despite Foley's plea to the representatives to put aside their passions and divisions and make the budget process work, his speech was overshadowed by representatives who were mad. They were furious at the White House staff for its aggressive role in the summit, at the president for breaking his no-taxes pledge, and at Democrats such as Foley who would cut Medicare so much.

After four and a half hours of debate, at 1:20 A.M. on the morning of October 5, the House rejected the budget deal on a roll-call vote, 254 against and 179 in favor.

Although Foley was greatly disappointed by the vote on the summit package, he calmly accepted the criticism of the House and decided to push on. "I am a servant of the House," he said, "and I accept their judgment. We're not through yet. This is not the end of the world."[13]

The next morning, after a few hours of sleep, Foley was back at the Capitol, talking and listening to representatives. Although he conferred with President Bush, with Sununu and Darman, this time he attacked the problem the old way. Instead of working with House Republicans, who disagreed sharply among themselves over raising taxes, Democrats would craft a package they could support.

Meanwhile the public had become bitter and frustrated with the drawn-out process. President Bush closed the national parks for a day, and the press kept asking when a budget would be ready. Many representatives were worried about the elections coming up in the first week of November and resentful they couldn't adjourn and go home to campaign.

The plan that emerged over the next two weeks increased taxes for higher-income Americans instead of sharply increasing taxes on gas and fuel. It eased the cuts on Medicare. After passing both houses of Congress, the bill's final details were worked out by a House and Senate conference committee.

The resulting deficit reduction plan covers the years from 1991 to 1995 and reduces the annual deficit to less than $100 billion by fiscal year 1995. The plan puts caps on appropriations bills, so that Congress can decide how to allocate money among categories but not how much to spend. It imposes a tough pay-as-you-go policy. Any proposed tax cuts or increases in spending must be budget-neutral; they must not upset the balance of income or expenses.

The agreement was a triumph for the Democrats and for Foley's patient, flexible approach. In victory, Foley gave credit to the entire House. "We ought to have some credit for the fact that this is not an agreeable or easy job to do," Foley said. "It's courageous. It's heroic in some ways that the members of Congress can, in a representative government system, stand up immediately before an election and do unpopular things."

He staunchly defended the unwieldy democratic process. "People ought to take some hope from that process instead of dumping all over it, instead of saying that it isn't quite as tidy as some think it ought to be."[14].

Deliberations in the House have never been tidy. Foley's defense of the process is but the latest from Speakers who have acted in the belief that, however untidy, democracy must continue to address and resolve the important issues of their time.

‖2‖

HENRY CLAY AND SLAVERY

*"I go for honorable
compromise wherever
it can be made."*

When Henry Clay was elected Speaker of the House in 1811, the House was a smaller, simpler version of Tom Foley's House. Only 142 representatives from seventeen states assembled in the Capitol, arriving on horseback, in carriages, stagecoach, or packet boat. Convening in November, they usually adjourned by March, avoiding the hot summers in Washington, D.C. They were paid $6 a day; they had no offices, and they wrote laws with quill pens.

The six Speakers before Clay merely presided. Beginning with Frederick A. C. Muhlenberg of Pennsylvania in 1789, the Speaker was an impartial moderator, seldom speaking his own mind, much like the Speaker in the English House of Commons. On important issues, the House usually followed the policies of the presidents—George Washington, John Adams, Thomas Jefferson, and James Madison. The real power was with the man who had the president's ear. Every issue was discussed by the House as a whole, and temporary committees were formed only as needed.

Young Henry Clay, from the bustling frontier state of Kentucky, changed all that. Clay represented a new generation, sons of the Revolution rather than fathers of the Revolution. He was not so tied to the way things had always been done, so he felt free to change the unwritten rules. Elected Speaker his first day in the House, at the relatively young age of thirty-four, Clay was the most powerful public man in the land for the next fourteen years. The issue that matured him, that dominated his life and established his great reputation as a compromiser, was the westward expansion of slavery.

HARRY OF THE WEST

Clay himself was a slaveholder. After growing up in Virginia, he moved to the frontier town of Lexington, Kentucky, in 1797, where he acquired land and built a law practice and a political following.

By 1802, Clay owned five slaves, and he soon bought more to help grow corn, rye, and hemp and breed horses at his country home of Ashland. Kentucky was south of the Ohio River, a dividing line between slave and free states.

The West offered plenty of opportunity for an articulate young man with Clay's social skills and personal charm. His political career began when Kentuckians elected him to the legislature. Legislators then appointed him to fill an unexpired term in the U.S. Senate, although at twenty-nine he was one year too young, according to the Constitution. For a while Clay alternated between the Kentucky legislature and the U.S. Senate. He soon decided, however, that the solemnity of the Senate suited his temperament less than the rough-and-tumble atmosphere of the House, to which he was elected in 1811. Clay came into the 12th Congress with sixty-nine other new members.

"Harry of the West" carried to Washington the main issue agitating Kentuckians—Britain's continued treatment of the new nation like a colony. Westerners, in particular, resented Indian uprisings they thought were instigated by the British and British meddling with commerce along the Mississippi River, which was so important to the new states west of the Appalachians. President Madison, they thought, was reacting too timidly.

Many of the new representatives shared Clay's fierce nationalism. Born after the signing of the Declaration of Independence, they were well-educated lawyers from the newest states in the South or from the frontier regions, Kentucky, Tennessee, and Ohio. Because many of the older members had not been reelected, and no seniority system had been established, they had a rare opportunity to establish a "young boys'" network.

Clay stood out among the newcomers. The personality of the state suited the personality of the man. He was a hard-drinking gambler who believed in settling insults with duels, but he was also charming and skilled at oratory. When he talked, his face would become animated, his blue-gray eyes would flash, and his six-foot stature radiated self-confidence.[1]

After dinner, seated beside the fire at Mrs. Dawson's boarding house on Capitol Hill, Clay talked with other freshmen congressmen about their anti-British views. They were willing, even eager, to fight a second war of independence if necessary, earning them the label of War Hawks. When the session opened in November 1811, the War Hawks elected Clay Speaker. His acceptance speech promised to facilitate the transaction of business "in the most agreeable manner."[2]

MR. CLAY'S WAR

In his opening message to Congress, President Madison urged the legislators to prepare the country for war with Great Britain. Clay and the War Hawks needed little urging.

"What are we to gain by war?" Clay asked. "What

are we not to lose by peace? Commerce, character, a nation's best treasure, honor!"[3] Honor was not the only goal, however. Nationalists had their eyes on territory: Canada, Florida, and more of North America.

Immediately Clay began organizing the House for war. Clay took over conduct of foreign policy—normally the role of the president and his secretary of state—greatly increasing the Speaker's power as he did. Since most major measures were discussed and voted on by all the members meeting as a Committee of the Whole, the Speaker could control the deliberations. He was able to push through legislative acts for defense and appropriations.

As he did, Clay also found it necessary to expand the number of standing committees. In the first twenty years, a committee had sometimes been appointed to work out the details of a particular bill, but the committee was usually disbanded when its work was finished. Only a few standing committees on topics that regularly came before the House—like appropriations—had been established. Clay increased the number of standing committees and decided that he would choose the chairs. He appointed ardent nationalists who would treat appropriations or war preparations bills favorably.

Clay not only took leadership on national issues but he also reformed the House's disorderly behavior. Since there were no limits on debate, members could talk for hours on any subject. In self-defense, representatives would drown out a colleague they didn't want to hear by talking among themselves in loud tones, banging on their desks, or coughing. John Randolph of Virginia was in the habit of striding into the House in hunting clothes with his hound dogs at his heels.

Young Harry began enforcing the rules. If a member was out of order, he was firmly instructed to take his seat. Members asleep at their desks were told to wake up or go home. Feet had to be placed under instead of on desks, and the doorkeeper was ordered to take out Randolph's dogs. That action prompted Randolph to denounce Clay as a "boy dictator."[4]

To halt the ramblings of long-winded representatives, Clay introduced the technique of "moving the previous question." As soon as a member said, "I move the previous question," debate was cut off and an immediate vote taken.

One gentleman from Virginia complained when his speech was cut off. "You, sir, speak for the present generation, but I speak for posterity," he told the Speaker.

"Yes," Clay responded, "and you seem resolved to speak until the arrival of your audience."[5]

As Speaker, Clay did not remove himself from debate but spoke often on issues and always voted. After preparing himself carefully for a speech, "the Great Kentuckian" used the control and power of his voice to sway his listeners, always seeming to know just what to say to appeal to them. He considered himself not the umpire but the leader of the House, the "boldest of Speakers," according to Mary Follett, who wrote the first history of the position.[6]

When the War of 1812 did start, it was known as "Mr. Clay's War" because of his leadership in preparing for it. For the three years it lasted, Clay did everything he could, short of actually fighting, to make the war successful, but it did not go well. The British burned Washington, D.C., and trashed the Capitol, forcing the House to meet in a government office converted from a hotel. Americans under General Andrew Jackson finally won a great battle at New Orleans, but unknown to both armies, the peace treaty had already been signed in Ghent.

SLAVERY IN THE WEST

Clay resigned from Congress to represent the United States in the peace negotiations. When he was reelected

Although the United States entered the War of 1812 with high hopes for victory, the British burned Washington, D.C., and for a while the House of Representatives had to meet in a converted hotel.

and returned to the House in December 1815, he was again elected Speaker. After the war, settlers were rushing west of the Appalachians into land in Indiana, Mississippi, Illinois, and Alabama. Always a nationalist, Clay wanted to be sure the new states that were forming would be tied economically to the nation. He advocated the American System, a system of protection for manufacturers and internal improvements such as road building. He wanted to extend the National Road as far west as the Mississippi River to aid the flow of goods and people.

This same westward movement caused the problem that turned Clay from "the Great Kentuckian" into "the Great Compromiser." As slaveholders moved west in search of new, fertile land, they took their slaves with them. The westward expansion of slavery aroused the hostility of Northerners and dominated public debate from 1819 until 1861. For forty years, Clay's leadership postponed a great civil war over slavery.

The issue came before the House in 1819 when one of the newly settled territories applied for admission to the Union. After the War of 1812, Missouri had been settled by thousands of slaveholders and their slaves working wheat and cotton plantations. The property-holding voters of the territory wanted to enter the Union as a slaveholding state.

That raised a troubling question. The line dividing slave and free states began with the Mason-Dixon Line, which divided Delaware and Maryland. When extended westward, the natural line was the Ohio River as far west as the Mississippi; slavery was prohibited in states north of the Ohio. Missouri was almost wholly north of the line if the line were extended west of the Mississippi, but it was also part of the Louisiana Purchase, where slavery had existed before the land was purchased from France. History and geography were at odds.

The question divided the House by sections, too. Southerners wanted to be free to move west with their slaves, but Northerners feared the competition of slave labor when they too moved west. Admitting Missouri as a slaveholding state would upset the political balance between North and South in Congress. After the admission of Indiana in 1816, Mississippi in 1817, Illinois in 1818, and Alabama in 1819, there were eleven free states and eleven slave states, giving them equal representation in the Senate. In the House, free states had 105 members and slave states 81. Outnumbered in the House, the South did not want to lose equal representation in the Senate.

Northerners felt, however, that the South already had more representation than it was entitled to. Twenty of the seats the South held in Congress and twenty of its electoral votes in the election of presidents came from including slaves in the population count even though they could not vote. (According to the three-fifths compromise adopted at the writing of the Constitution, three-fifths of the slave population of a state would count toward determining the state's electoral votes and number of representatives.) Northerners, particularly those in the Northeast, feared that the admission of Missouri would strengthen the voting power of the South; they wanted to take power away from the "Virginia Dynasty" that had produced four of the first five presidents.

As a "Westerner," Clay had a third point of view, that new states should not be subject to any more restrictions than the old states. When the House was deciding whether to allow the territory of Arkansas to be organized with slavery in 1819, Clay had cast the deciding vote allowing no restrictions on slavery. As a slaveholder, he generally took the moderate Southern position that it was up to the states themselves to gradually abolish slavery. With that goal in mind, he had called for a constitutional convention in Kentucky in 1799 to adopt a plan of gradual emancipation. He advised Missourians to do the same.

Meanwhile he saw a possible opening in the deadlock. A few Northerners feared that the country would be divided not only by slave and by free states but by political parties, too. They thought that the Federalist party, which had lost power when it did not support the War of 1812, would become strong again and predominate in the North. Democrats would prevail in the South. Some Northern Democrats were willing to side with the Southern Democrats in order to prevent the resurgence of the Federalists. Clay worked on that minority of Northerners to come up with a compromise.

THE "MISERY DEBATES"

Three torturous debates preceded the eventual compromise, known as the Missouri Compromise. The first began on February 13, 1819, when the House considered a petition that had been presented to Henry Clay asking for the admission of Missouri as a state. Immediately James Tallmadge of New York moved to amend the bill to admit Missouri to prohibit the further introduction of slaves into the state. His amendment would also free all slave children born in the state when they reached the age of fifteen.

Northern supporters of the amendment said that slavery was immoral and its expansion should be stopped. Southerners responded that Congress had no power to restrict slavery in the states, that only the states had the right to do that. They conceded that slavery was wrong, but they said emancipation was impractical. The bill as amended passed the House, where the North had a majority, but was voted down in the Senate, where the sections were equally represented.

Reconvening in December, in new chambers built after the burning of 1814, the House was still at an impasse. The "Misery [Missouri] Debates" continued for weeks to the exclusion of all other congressional business. "The Missouri subject monopolizes all our conversation, all our thoughts and for three weeks at least to come will all our time," the Speaker wrote to a friend in January 1820. "Nobody seems to think or care about anything else."[7]

The subject aroused immense public interest. Spectators, including women and Negroes, crowded the galleries, sometimes overflowing onto the House floor. (Annoyed by the presence of women, John Randolph suggested they go home.) In a chamber lighted by a huge chandelier with a hundred candles, the orations went on late into the night. The air, heated by stoves that had replaced the fireplaces, grew stale.

"As one side or other of the question preponderates," Clay wrote, the Negro population of Washington, D.C. "rejoice or are depressed."[8]

Great tension infused the debate as the words *civil war, disunion,* and *bloodshed* were freely flung about. When a Northern delegate took the moral position that one man could not legally enslave another, the slaveholding representatives "gnawed their lips and clenched their fists."[9]

"If you persist," Thomas Cobb of Georgia told Northerners, "the Union will be dissolved. You have kindled a fire which all the waters of the ocean cannot put out, which seas of blood can only extinguish."

"If a dissolution of the Union must take place, let it be so!" fiercely responded Tallmadge. "If civil war, which gentlemen so threaten, must come, I can only say, let it come!"[10]

"How can you expect to persuade such men?" wrote another.[11]

The talk of disunion caused alarm beyond the walls of the Capitol. John Quincy Adams, secretary of state, wrote, "I take it for granted that the present question is a mere preamble—a title-page to a great, tragic volume."[12]

Clay experienced the conflict within himself. Although he admitted slavery was evil, the "deepest stain upon the character of our country,"[13] his own holdings had increased to sixty slaves and he bought and sold them as needed. He favored effective fugitive slave laws, and he offered rewards for his own runaway slaves. On the other hand, he freed several of his slaves as a reward for faithful service.

At first in the debate Clay vigorously championed the Southern point of view. With the threat of sectional conflict hanging over the House, however, he modified his position. He had ambitions to be president. Preservation of the Union was more important than pushing the Southern view. As the rhetoric and oratory continued to threaten the Union's very survival, he turned his great energies to searching for a compromise on the Missouri question.

An opportunity arose in the midst of the debate when Maine petitioned Congress late in 1819 to be admitted as a free state. Speaker Clay told Northerners they would not be able to admit Maine until they admitted Missouri, "free of condition," meaning no restriction on slavery.

Early in February 1820 came a proposal from Jesse B. Thomas of Illinois that was eventually to form the compromise. Thomas suggested admitting Maine as a free state and Missouri as a slave state and leaving Arkansas and Oklahoma open to future settlement by slaveholders. In the future, however, north of a line at latitude 36° 30', slavery would be prohibited. This line would run along the southern border of Missouri, leaving this slaveholding chunk as an exception above the line.

Clay immediately supported the Thomas amendment, and moderates rallied to it. Southerners found the proposal acceptable. Northerners did not, but Clay thought a few might be willing to go along for the sake of preserving the Union.

On February 8 he spoke for four hours, directing all his oratorical skills at wavering Northerners. His mobile face and body twisted "in the most dreadful scowls and contortions" to argue against restrictions on slavery in

Missouri.[14] Clay particularly spoke to Pennsylvania's Democratic representatives, who had usually allied with the South but were supporting New England and the Federalists on the slavery issue. Thomas Forrest, a Quaker, was a senior member of the delegation. A newspaper reporter wrote that Clay "wielded the powers of pathos in a manner so sublime and touching that the old man himself [Forrest] became restless and half the House were in tears."[15] If all else failed, Clay threatened to go home and raise troops to defend Missouri.

Despite his speech, the House rejected the Thomas amendment. Instead they approved an antislavery amendment introduced by John W. Taylor. Meanwhile the Senate had approved the dual admission of Maine and Missouri with the addition of the Thomas amendment. A conference committee, with members from both houses, was formed to try to resolve the deadlock.

On March 2 the conference committee took the Senate view and recommended to the House that the Thomas amendment be added and the Taylor amendment eliminated. With four Northerners absent and fourteen more voting with the majority, the antislavery proviso was eliminated, 90 to 87. Then the Thomas amendment was passed, 134 to 42.

The compromise was not yet assured, however. The night after the vote against the anti-slavery amendment, the eccentric John Randolph was on his feet demanding a reconsideration, which any member who voted with the majority may do. Randolph hoped that by reopening the debate, the whole deal might be undone. With everyone exhausted and one member seriously ill, Clay told Randolph his motion would be in order the next day.

The next morning Randolph rose to offer his motion to reconsider, but Clay delayed the motion until the routine business of the morning was finished. While the House went through the procedure of receiving and referring petitions, Clay quickly signed the compromise bill and sent it off with the clerk of the House to the Senate. Finally recognizing Randolph, Clay told him that the bill was already out of the House's jurisdiction and could not be reconsidered. Randolph moved to censure the clerk for his hasty action, but the House refused to consider the motion and the Speaker was upheld.

Maine was admitted to the Union that day, and the people of Missouri were authorized to form a constitution and a state government with no restrictions on slavery. Thus was the first compromise made, with Clay's firm hand pushing it along.

Issues in Congress seldom die quietly. The Missouri Compromise had passed by only a narrow margin, and the majority of Northerners still opposed it and looked for ways to reopen the debate. Twice more in the 16th Congress Clay had to defend the compromise before Missouri could actually be admitted to the Union.

THE SECOND AND THIRD MISSOURI DEBATES

Over the summer, Henry Clay resigned as Speaker to attend to business affairs at home. It took twenty-two ballots to elect a replacement acceptable to both sides. Then when Missouri submitted its proposed constitution in the fall of 1820, the document contained several provisions offensive to Northerners. One provision prohibited the entry of free Negroes and mulattoes into the state. Free Negroes were feared for their potentially disruptive influence on slaves and for the competition of their labor. Another provision forbade the legislature to emancipate slaves without the consent of their owners. The proposed constitution was rejected in December, and the "Misery Debates" were reopened.

The second phase of the debate came with the counting and reporting of the electoral votes for the 1820 presidential election. President James Monroe had been clearly reelected, but the question was raised whether

Missouri's electoral votes should be counted in the returns since its constitution had not been approved. Clay, who returned to the House in mid-January 1821, was appointed to a joint committee of the Senate and House to consider the problem.

The committee recommended a "have it both ways" solution. If Missouri's votes were challenged and if counting Missouri's votes would not affect the outcome of the election, the presiding officer should announce two sets of returns, one with Missouri's vote and one without.

Clay presented the compromise recommendation and it was approved on February 14, the very day the count was to be made. The Senate was invited over for the formal count, and the chamber was jammed with spectators expecting excitement and opposition.

When the presiding officer reached Missouri in the count, the predicted challenge was made, and Southerners were greatly offended. The House broke into such pandemonium that the more stately senators decided to withdraw.

With what was described as "great force and dignity," Clay claimed the floor and moved to delay the voting on the challenge until after the count.[16] The Senate was invited back again. Amid repeated shouts of "Order!" the count was finished by candlelight. Monroe was elected, with or without Missouri's vote, and the issue was avoided.

The third debate occurred when the subject returned to Missouri's constitution. Although Clay was not Speaker, he again led the forces for compromise. Opponents of approving the state's constitution said that its exclusion of free Negroes violated that part of the federal constitution that guarantees the same privileges and immunities to all American citizens. Weren't free Negroes entitled to these rights? Missouri's supporters said that the courts should decide whether the exclusion was constitutional. After all, several other states already in the Union also denied admission to free Negroes.

At first Clay argued the Southern position. When the debate continued for days, however, with tension again increasing, he suggested a joint conference committee of thirteen members of the House and Senate to come up with a compromise.

As a committee member, Clay used all his charm to forge a compromise amendment. How did he succeed? Describing Clay's style, one member commented, "He uses no threats or abuse but all is mild, humble and persuasive—he begs, entreats, adjures, supplicates and beseeches us to have mercy upon the people of Missouri."[17] The committee recommended that Missouri be admitted under the condition that the state would not pass any law preventing "any citizens" of states from coming and settling there. The ambiguous phrase was "any citizens," since it avoided the question of whether that included free blacks.

After a heated debate, the recommendation was defeated by three votes. A majority of Northerners then voted to undo the entire compromise by forcing Missouri to abolish slavery before being admitted. That failed by a larger margin.

"This distracting question," said one, "this ominous and ill-boding question" said another, once again threatened to halt all congressional action and divide the Union.[18] Time was running out before the current session would recess in March.

"There is one man, and only one man, who can save the Union. That man is Henry Clay," intoned John Randolph, the same Randolph who had called Clay a boy dictator and taunted him to a duel. "I know he has the power. I believe he will be found to have the patriotism and firmness equal to the occasion."[19]

Ever attentive to political winds, Clay sensed another opening for compromise. On February 22, word came of the ratification of the Florida treaty, which sold Florida and all other Spanish-claimed land east of the Mississippi to the United States. This treaty also said that slavery would not spread to new areas in the old Southwest. Thinking this provision might reassure Northerners, Clay decided to try his charm and persuasiveness once more on wavering representatives.

Clay moved that a new joint committee be chosen to consider the Missouri question. Moreover, he suggested that the members not be appointed by the Speaker but be elected by ballot. He had his ballot ready. He circulated a list of moderates and Northerners who might be won over to compromise, and most of his people were selected.

The committee's deliberations began on a Saturday, when Clay converted one New Jersey representative, then continued through Sunday, when he converted two more Pennsylvania representatives to his position. On Monday, February 26, the committee presented to the House essentially the same proposal Clay's earlier committee had made. The Missouri legislature must solemnly agree that the state's constitution and laws should never be used to take away from citizens entering the state the rights and privileges guaranteed to them under the federal Constitution.

Before the committee reported, Clay had polled every member to ask how they would vote. "Now, gentlemen," he told the members, "we do not want a proposition carried here by a small majority, thereupon reported to the House, and rejected. How will you vote Mr. A? and you Mr. B? and so on."[20] The committee's report was nearly unanimous and the recommended amendment passed, 87 to 81. The Missouri legislature defiantly did as it was told, and the state was admitted on August 10, 1821. Finally, the issue of Missouri was settled.

Although the westward expansion of slavery had threatened the Union, the Missouri Compromise held it together for thirty more years. It was no small achievement. Clay's reputation grew as a result of his leadership. Dinners were held in his honor. Thomas Hart Benson, the historian, gave him the title the "Great Pacificator." One newspaper attributed the legislation's success to "the very extraordinary exertions of an extraordinary man" and to his "grand committees."[21] Even a rival, John Quincy Adams, admitted the crisis had brought Clay's talents into full play.

What were those talents? Clay was an eloquent defender of the art of compromise. He said his success came from not stating his own opinions in too strong a fashion, in not taking a stand from which he could not give a little in order to gain something. "I go for honorable compromise wherever it can be made. . . . All legislation, all government, all society is founded upon the principle of mutual concession, politeness, comity, courtesy; upon these everything is based."[22]

THE COMPROMISE OF 1850

Listening to the ominous debate on slavery as he neared the end of his life, Thomas Jefferson had seen the future: "This momentous question, like a fire bell in the night, awakened and filled me with terror," he wrote. "I considered it at once as the knell of the Union."[23]

Clay was Speaker of the House until 1825, setting a record for length in that office that was not broken until the twentieth century. After serving as secretary of state from 1825 to 1829, he was elected by the Kentucky legislature to serve in the Senate from 1831 to 1842 and again in 1849. Although he had hopes for the presidency in 1824, 1832, 1840, 1844, and 1848, he never achieved that goal. Instead he was given one last chance to fashion a compromise that would save the Union.

In 1850 the Great Pacificator was seventy-three years old. His cheeks were hollower, his head bald on top. At

Henry Clay tried five times to win the presidency but was unsuccessful on each occasion. This cartoon depicts the Whig Party's betrayal of Henry Clay as presidential candidate.

times he looked quite old and shriveled, but a worthy cause would bring alive his smile, his wit, and his love of conversation.

The cause in 1850 was the same as it had been in 1820: fervid disagreements over the extension of slavery west. The Mexican-American War of 1848 brought new land into the United States—territory that became California, New Mexico, and Arizona. The Gold Rush propelled thousands of miners and others to California, which adopted an antislavery constitution and applied for admission to the Union.

The South again saw a threat to the balance of free and slave states in the Senate and threatened secession. The North saw a moral issue in any extension of slavery to territories where it had not existed before. The constant division over unity was fraying the delicate fiber of unity. In 1848 the 30th Congress had ended with fistfights in both houses. In 1849 the House needed fifty-three ballots before a Speaker could be elected. Then representatives spent days hurling taunts and insults before electing a doorkeeper. While President Zachary Taylor's message to Congress in December 1849 recommended the admission of California, John C. Calhoun of South Carolina threatened to lead the Southern states to secession.

Once more, Clay was alarmed by the clamoring toward disunion. Even though he had a very bad cough, the elder statesman set out on a stormy January night in 1850 to call on Daniel Webster, a senator from the North who favored the admission of California as a free state. For an hour Clay talked to Webster, detailing his ideas for a compromise that would satisfy the majority who wanted to admit California but prevent the ultras from the South from seceding. At the end of the hour, Webster promised to support the compromise in principle.

Clay's plan consisted of eight resolutions: the admission of California, the organization of other territory ac-

With the United States' victory during the Mexican-American War, the territories of New Mexico, Arizona, and California were acquired. Debate then ensued over the question of the introduction of slavery into these lands.

quired from Mexico without restriction on slavery, abolition of the slave trade in the District of Columbia, a more effective fugitive slave law, and a resolution denying Congress the power to interfere with the interstate slave trade.

After gathering support from other senators who wanted to preserve the Union, Clay feebly climbed the long flight of steps leading to the Capitol on February 5. The Senate chamber was crowded with those who wanted to hear him make one of the most important speeches of his life. Their emotions and the overheating of the room raised the temperature to 100 degrees. Clay spoke for nearly three hours, disdaining, he said, any oratorical display on such a serious occasion. Instead he appealed to the reason and patriotic feelings of Americans, especially their love for the Union. He defended each resolution of the compromise he had suggested, asking both sides to make concessions.

After the Senate adjourned to allow him to finish the next day, he closed by stating his solemn belief that no state had the right to secede and that if the South did secede, a disastrous civil war would follow. If it did, he hoped that "I may not survive to behold the sad and heart-rending spectacle."[24]

Compromises are not made with one speech. The real work of negotiating had only begun, and it fell to men of a new generation, such as Stephen Douglas of Illinois. William Seward of New York and Salmon Chase took up the opposition to compromise. They attacked slavery and the fugitive slave law in particular. Compromise would be a surrender of principle, they said, one of Clay's "sneaking compromises." Seward called Clay's plan "magnificent humbug," and Clay himself the "prince of humbugs, charlatans and traitors."[25]

Nevertheless, Clay was appointed to try a familiar solution: a committee of thirteen was formed from both parties and both sections of the country to consider and

As president, Zachary Taylor pushed for the admission of California into the Union as a non-slave state.

present an omnibus bill, a bill that covered everything. The committee reported an omnibus bill with everything Clay had proposed earlier except the slave trade provision.

The debate continued into the summer, well past the normal time to adjourn for a week to allow the heavy carpets and draperies to be removed. Clay said he did not care about having the matting put down; he would be content with the carpet all summer, and so the talk went on through the blazing heat.

President Zachary Taylor was one of those opposing a compromise, but on a blistering July 4 he drank too much ice water and iced milk and ate too many cherries during the festivities. That evening he became ill and developed typhoid, dying five days later. When Taylor died and Millard Fillmore succeeded him, an obstacle to compromise was eliminated.

Clay made his last great plea later that month, but on July 31 he watched as sections of the omnibus bill were stripped away one by one until only one provision was left. Finally worn out by the effort, Clay left for Newport, Rhode Island, to rest and bathe in the sea.

Stephen Douglas took up the leadership effort and guided each part of the bill through with a bloc of Northern and Southern moderates supporting it. When Clay returned in late August, he took charge of the final bill abolishing the slave trade in the District of Columbia. It passed the Senate on September 15 and the House on September 17, and the Compromise of 1850 was approved. The spirit of moderation that finally prevailed postponed for another ten years what became an inevitable conflict.

Looking back on the compromise, Clay said, "If anyone desires to know the leading and paramount object of my public life, the preservation of the Union will furnish him the key."[26] Fortunately, he did not live to see the war that claimed more than half a million lives.

> In 1850, when debate over California's admission into the Union as a free state led to threats of secession from Southern representatives, Henry Clay was asked to help arrange a compromise.

Only when the war was over and the nation reunited would strong Speakers emerge again. Not all would follow the moderate style of the Great Compromiser, but they learned from him how to assert the power of the Speaker to maintain order and to push along new issues that once again aroused passion in the country and in Congress.

|3|

THOMAS BRACKETT REED AND THE RULES

"The best system is to have one party govern and the other party watch."

Thomas Brackett Reed was a large man, "a huge six-foot gelatinous walrus of a man," said historian William Allen White.[1]

"Big head, big brain," Sam Rayburn said.[2] When Reed looked down from the Speaker's dais, he was even more imposing. On a January day in 1890, Reed was presiding calmly from the chair, gavel in hand, as bedlam erupted on the House floor.

The bedlam was caused by Reed, who had been elected Speaker of the 51st Congress by a very thin Republican majority. When he called the House to order to consider its first item of business—a disputed congressional election—the Democratic minority had pulled a familiar obstructionist tactic. It had called for a quorum, a count to see if a majority of the members of the House were actually present to conduct business.

The necessary quorum was 165, the precise number of Republicans in the House, but when the roll was called, only 163 members responded. All the Democrats present remained silent, hoping to sidetrack whatever business the Speaker and the Republican majority hoped to accomplish that day. Without a quorum, no votes could be taken.

Reed knew all about such tactics. He had been in the House for thirteen years, since 1877, and most of the time he had been in the minority party. When he came to the House, after several years' service as legislator and attorney general in Maine, he quickly understood that procedure was everything as far as accomplishment was concerned. He also learned that most representatives were not even listened to: "Distinction won in the fields of endeavor will gain a man a hearing for the first time, but not afterward. If he wishes to talk and be listened to, he had better have something to say and know how to say it."[3]

So Reed concentrated on becoming a man worth listening to. He read widely, spending many free hours in secondhand bookstores looking for rare publications. When he was informed sufficiently to speak on an issue, he revealed a nasal Maine drawl that could be irritating to the members, but his sarcastic wit and quick tongue kept their attention. Many of his colleagues, he said, "never opened their mouths without subtracting from the sum of human knowledge."[4] Unlike those unfortunate colleagues, Reed was always well prepared, and his speeches were said to "bristle with points." No one yawned while he was on his feet.[5]

Fine speeches aside, any representative's chances of pushing through a favorite piece of legislation were quite slim in the late nineteenth century. Despite the changes Clay had made, the House floor was frequently in disorder and subsequently known as the "Bear Yard." Representatives fell asleep with their feet on their desks, many chewed tobacco, others pared their fingernails, and some were drunk. The House spent about $400 a year just cleaning the spittoons placed beside each member's desk. One Speaker, J. Warren Keifer of Ohio, carried a pistol in his pocket when he presided, to deal with violence if necessary.

A ponderous pace matched the bearlike behavior. When Congress first met in 1789, the members represented a population of 3 million. By the last quarter of the nineteenth century, they represented 60 million people. Westward expansion and the development of farming and ranching, along with the growth of industrialism and an urban working class, had raised economic issues with strong social implications.

Yet the House had been stalled for years, paralyzed by rules full of "intricacies and secrets."[6] Usually members were unable to complete even a tenth of the legislation that was introduced. At the end of each session Reed had seen a mad scramble to pass a few bills. "We undertake to run Niagara [Falls] through a quill," he remarked.[7] It was a situation he intended to change.

Attempts at reform had already been made. In the summer of 1879 a committee of five met to revise and simplify the rules. They recommended giving more authority to the Speaker and to the Rules Committee. Henceforth, the Rules Committee would be composed of three majority members, including the Speaker as chair, and two minority members. The Rules Committee would control the flow of bills to the floor for consideration. It could limit debate or completely block consideration of a bill. Because Reed's leadership skills were recognized, he was appointed to the Rules Committee in 1881 after only four years in the House.

Despite these changes, the minority could still keep any action at all from occurring by using the filibuster and movements to adjourn. The calendar became unmanageably congested with bills considered in the order they were placed on the calendar rather than in order of importance. During the 50th Congress—from 1887 to 1888—the entire legislative process came close to breaking down. There were over 400 roll call votes that session, 86 on one bill alone, with no action taken. "It is a magnificent tribute to us, thus spending one whole month of our time calling over our own names," Reed complained.[8]

One member staged an eight-day filibuster using dilatory motions and roll calls in an effort to force the House to consider a bill organizing the Territory of Oklahoma. The press called it "filibustering gone mad."[9] Thus the public and the members of the House were ready for reform when Reed was elected Speaker and decided to challenge the obstructionist tactics of the minority.

THE DISAPPEARING QUORUM DISAPPEARS

Gazing down impassively from the dais on January 29, 1890, Reed steeled himself to confront the Democrats. When they refused to answer the quorum call, he announced in a firm voice, "The Chair directs the clerk to record the names of the following members present and refusing to vote."[10] Then he began naming the representatives he saw. As he did, pandemonium broke out at the revolutionary action he was taking. Democrats swarmed to the well, the sergeant at arms waved the mace (symbol of the Speaker's authority) in the air, and Reed stood calmly behind his desk. Every time he called a name, catcalls were shouted and fists were shaken in the air. As the uproar subsided, the Speaker would call another name.

"I am not here," cried one representative when named.

"I deny your right, Mr. Speaker, to count me as present," declared another member who wanted to read from the parliamentary law on the subject of quorums.[11]

"The Chair is making a statement of the fact that the gentleman from Kentucky is present," Reed wryly responded. "Does he deny it?"[12]

For three days the outcry continued, but Reed remained unruffled. Democrats began trying to get out of his sight by hiding under their desks or bolting for the doors. They called him a czar, a despot, and a tyrant.

When the House was quiet long enough for the Speaker to make a longer statement, he explained the constitutional basis for his opinion that a quorum consisted of those present, whether they were voting or not. The Constitution gave the House the power to compel the attendance of absent members, he said. They could be found and forced to come to the chamber. If they couldn't also be counted as part of a quorum, what good was their attendance? He maintained that the Constitution merely provided for attendance and said nothing about not voting because attendance was enough for a quorum. After he explained his decision, Reed said that it could be overruled by the House on appeal.

Reed had taken a great gamble in standing firm on the "disappearing quorum." If merely one Republican decided to side with the Democrats on the issue, he could be overruled. Reed had told at least one good friend that he would resign from the speakership and retire from the House if that happened. The 51st Congress would accomplish nothing, he knew, if the delaying tactics of the minority were allowed to obstruct the will of the majority. Indeed he labeled the minority's tactic of not voting "the weapon of anarchy."[13]

"Our government is founded on the doctrine that if 100 think one way and 101 think the other, the 101 are right," he said. "It is the old doctrine that the majority must govern. . . . If the majority do not govern, the minority will. . . ."[14]

When the House did vote on his ruling, after much filibustering by the Democrats, every Republican stood with Reed, and his decision was sustained. Then on February 2, the House voted by a majority of one to seat the member whose election had been disputed. Finally the House could proceed with the rest of its business. A few months later, the Supreme Court upheld Reed's ruling on quorum counting.

In his first month as Speaker, Reed continued his parliamentary revolution. Motions that were obviously dilatory, he decided, could be ruled out of order. For example, when a representative presented a motion to adjourn or to take a recess in the middle of important debate, Reed ruled the motion dilatory, made with the intent to obstruct the business of the House.

A full set of "Reed's Rules" was reported to the House on February 5 by the Rules Committee. The rules included other changes that streamlined the consideration of legislation. The Speaker was given more power to deny recognition to a member who wished to speak. He would follow the precedent set by a previous Speaker of asking, "For what purpose does the gentleman rise?" If the purpose did not suit the Speaker, he could refuse recognition. Reed would also appoint chairs of the standing committees. He decided to add the chairs of the Ways and Means and Appropriations committees to the Rules Committee. With these two chairs and himself on the Rules Committee, they formed a steering committee for important legislation.

Reed's strong hand earned him the epithet of "czar," which gave cartoonists of the day ample opportunity for drawing crowns and scepters. Reed himself had a sense of humor about his power. An oft-repeated anecdote relates that one day Reed was asked by a constituent for a copy of the rules of the House. Mr. Reed sent him an autographed picture.

Despite the adoption of Reed's Rules, the minority continued to attempt to obstruct the majority whenever possible. At one point in a session, Reed ordered the doors locked to prevent Democrats from leaving when he began counting a quorum. Democrat C. Buckley Kilgore of Texas was so determined to leave he kicked out

Thomas Brackett Reed's knowledge of parliamentary procedure and his efficient use of constitutional law led to the creation of "Reed's Rules," which gave the Speaker greater power in setting the agenda for the House of Representatives.

the panels of a door leading into the lobby. The door crashed open, he went out, and a Republican who had been waiting outside came in with a damaged nose. No gain or loss in quorum.

PUTTING THE RULES TO WORK

What difference did Reed's challenge to the minority make? Why was he so determined that the majority—his Republican party—would prevail?

He firmly believed that parties could and should govern. "A good party," he wrote, "is better than the best man that ever lived."[15] Since the Civil War two strong parties had gradually emerged, the Democrats and the Republicans. The party winning the most seats in the biennial elections would elect a Speaker and attempt to put its legislative program through.

If the majority was unable to lead, as it had been, Reed considered that a deplorable situation. "Whenever the people have elected one party to take control of the House or the Senate, that party shall have both the power and the responsibility. If that is not the effect, what is the use of the election?" Reed asked.[16]

Less seriously, he claimed that "The best system is to have one party govern and the other party watch, and on general principles I think it would be better for us to govern and the Democrats to watch."[17] That's what he had in mind in 1890.

The Republicans had an agenda for governing, a legislative program that would support the rapid growth of the economy at the end of the nineteenth century. They wanted to encourage business, attract investors by maintaining a sound currency, protect industry with tariffs, and avoid government meddling. The Congresses of the 1880s and 1890s spent much of their sessions considering banking and currency, tariffs and taxes, and the regulation of private business.

On many of these issues, Congress was split between those who represented the industrial Northeast and Midwestern states like Ohio and Illinois, and those who represented the Far West and the Great Plains states. It was also split between business and workers, bankers and farmers, and railroad men and ranchers. All of the economic issues affected someone's pocketbook and overall well-being.

Reed was not a man with a cause, but he was a Republican from New England. He had never been a businessman, but he had been a lawyer. By and large his economic views were the same as the Republican party's. He sided with businessmen and New England manufacturers against farmers and workers. He sided with those who manufactured plows, harnesses, and shirts against those who bought them.

The issues that brought him to his feet to debate were primarily tariffs (taxes on goods imported into the country) and sound currency, paper money backed by gold. He stood solidly behind the gold standard and supported tariffs but did not consider them untouchable. On both issues he became the Republicans' spokesman. His vigor, his intellect, and his imposing size (250 to 275 pounds) commanded attention. When Reed spoke on an issue, Joe Cannon described it as crystallizing an idea, rolling it up with his hands into proper shape, and hurling it at the head of his opponent. Another Speaker after him, Champ Clark, described Reed's style as driving home his propositions "with the force of a pile driver."[18]

PROTECTING BUSINESS WITH THE TARIFF

Protectionism and its chief tool, the tariff, were debated frequently in the 1880s and 1890s as numerous bills were discussed, passed, and sometimes repealed. Congress was constantly tinkering with tariffs, raising them on some products and lowering them on others. "If anything seems to have been discussed until human nature can bear it no more, it is the tariff," Reed said in one of his speeches on the subject.[19]

Reed thought that protective tariffs were both necessary and beneficial. Placing a tax on manufactured goods from other countries would protect "infant industries" in the United States. He was opposed to free trade and "survival of the fittest" for businesses. On the other hand, he did not think government should intervene to protect farmers and workers. If protection of business resulted in higher prices for those who bought the goods, they would eventually benefit from the health of the economy and from jobs at higher wages. Thus Reed espoused an early version of the trickle-down theory.

Democrats thought otherwise. Grover Cleveland, a Democrat, had been elected president in 1884 at a time when the U.S. Treasury had a large surplus, so Cleveland urged cutting tariffs, the government's main source of income. American industries were strong enough, he said. Besides, protected industries didn't pay their workers any higher wages than other industries. High tariffs were just producing high prices for the public and high profits for business people, Cleveland argued.

He urged passage of the Mills bill, a free-trade measure and an attempt at tariff reform. It proposed to remove tariffs from some items, such as hemp, flax, lumber, and wool, and reduce the duty on pig iron.

Reed gave his first major speech on the tariff in 1888 when he presented the Republican case against the Mills bill. In his two-hour closing speech for the minority, he claimed that protective tariffs did not create monopolies and trusts. He recounted Aesop's fable of a dog carrying a shoulder of mutton in his jaws who saw his own reflection in a stream. The dog lost what he had when he opened his mouth to grab for more. Wanting to open the markets of the world to American products by reducing tariffs all around would be greedy, Reed said. Look how the ordinary people had benefited already during twenty-seven years of protection and marvelous economic growth. Let them keep what they had.[20]

Despite Reed's speech, the Mills bill passed the House, where the Democrats had a majority, but it died in the Republican-dominated Senate. Showing gratitude in the election that year, 1888, business gave large sums of money to the Republican candidate, Benjamin Harrison, who was elected. A small Republican majority was elected in the House, too, setting the stage for Reed to become Speaker and the Republicans to push their legislative program.

Once Reed's Rules were established in 1890, the 51st Congress proceeded to the issues Republicans felt they had been elected to address. At the top of the list was a generally pro-tariff tariff bill which removed the duty on sugar but placed new duties on other products. Reed used the "steering committee" of three he had created—himself, the chairman of Ways and Means and the chairman of Appropriations—to force the bill through. He was criticized, especially by Western members, for not allowing enough debate. The McKinley Tariff Act of 1890, on which Reed and the majority prevailed, would also become their undoing.

After securing the future of tariff revenues, the 51st Congress found itself with a surplus. In fact the 51st became known as the "billion-dollar Congress" for the amount of money it voted to spend, much of it on public works and a new steel navy.

Shortly after passage of the McKinley Tariff, however, a general increase in domestic prices occurred, and the tariff was blamed. The people held the Republicans responsible and voted for Democrats in the November election. The Democrats would become the majority party when the new House convened late in 1891. Angered by the rules changes Reed had made, Democrats declined to offer the customary resolution of thanks to the Speaker at the end of the session.

The new Democratic leadership of the 52nd and 53rd Congresses quickly reverted to the old rules, much to their eventual regret. As minority leader, Reed had no qualms whatsoever about dragging out the old obstructionist tactics. Faced with filibusters, quorum calls, and dilatory motions, and unable to produce a quorum from their own ranks, the Democrats were forced to count silent members, as Reed had done, to establish a quorum.

The issues Reed stood up for as minority leader were the same as they had been: sound finance and the tariff. In 1893 Reed made a speech urging repeal of the Sherman Silver Purchase Act. The act required the U.S. Treasury to buy almost the entire annual output of American silver mines to back the nation's currency. Because most of the Democrats and some Republicans favored the bill, he had been unable to stop it in the 51st Congress.

Silver mines in the West benefited greatly from the law. In 1893 Reed made a speech urging its repeal. The nation was going through a severe depression, and workers and farmers pleaded with the government to buy more silver. Reed argued that ups and downs in the economy were natural and that the world of business would settle itself. With Democratic president Grover Cleveland and Reed both on the same side, the act was repealed.

On tariffs the Democratic majority was more successful. In 1894 they pushed through the Wilson bill, which rolled back many of the tariffs raised by the McKinley Act. As ranking minority member of the Ways and Means Committee, Reed led the opposition and brilliantly defended protectionism as beneficial to the nation and causing a great rise in real wages. His speeches in opposition to the bill helped Republicans sweep the next election and bring him back to the speakership in 1895.

THE GAVEL OF SOUND FINANCE

Reed returned to the chair missing one of his trademarks. He had fallen asleep in the House barbershop, and the barber had waxed the points of his mustache. When the customer awoke and looked in the mirror, he was horrified: "Shave that mustache off. You've made me look like a darned catfish."[21]

Reed had much smoother second and third terms as Speaker from 1895 to 1899. There were Republicans in the presidency—Harrison and then McKinley—and much larger Republican majorities in the House. Reed began the session in 1895 with a new gavel to replace the one he had pounded to death in his previous term. The new gavel had bands of silver and gold representing bimetallism, part of the second bedrock issue for Republicans, sound finance.

"The proudest part of the proud record of the Republican Party has been its steadfast devotion to the cause of sound finance," Reed affirmed.[22] With Reed's Rules back in force, the Republicans were able to prevail on sound finance, which to them meant adherence to the gold standard, the backing of U.S. paper dollars with their equivalent value in gold bullion stored at Fort Knox. If the government didn't have enough bullion to support the paper money it issued, Republicans said, no one would respect the value of the dollar.

Farmers and workers, on the other hand, tended to be borrowers and consumers. They favored cheap money and free coinage, the coinage of both silver and gold with the government buying silver to keep it at a parity with gold. Farmers are often in debt for equipment, land, and supplies, and debts are easier to pay if the government supply of money grows. They also hoped farm prices would rise with cheap money. Republicans were opposed to free coinage and favored bimetallism, which set a fixed ratio of silver to gold, with gold having a higher value.

Free coinage was the main issue dividing the country in the 1896 campaign. Because of his leadership on sound finance, many thought Reed would be the best presidential nominee. The Republicans passed over him, however, in favor of William McKinley, who was more personable if less imposing than Reed. McKinley ran against William Jennings Bryan, whose Populist platform appealed to farmers, wage earners, and small business people. Bryan said that silver as well as gold should be used to back the dollar, but he and his position were defeated. Republicans received the support of big business, and McKinley won easily. Reed was elected Speaker again for the 1897–98 session.

Once more the first item on the agenda was revision of tariffs, the Dingley Tariff bill, but this time Reed took a more moderate approach. The sugar-refining monopoly wanted higher tariffs on sugar than the House bill granted. The monopoly persuaded the Senate to hold up the bill. To strengthen his negotiating position, Reed refused to make committee appointments until the Senate acted. Other Senate bills could not be sent to House committees for action. Finally the Senate acted near the end of the session. The Dingley Tariff passed with tariffs at levels acceptable to Reed.

He was not so successful on another issue that mattered to him. For the second time in the nineteenth century, Cubans were fighting for their independence from Spain. The second rebellion had started in February 1895 and had provoked harsh responses from a Spanish general sent to put it down. Early U.S. recognition of the Cuban rebels might have helped their cause, but a bill granting recognition was stalled because of Reed's abovementioned refusal to make committee appointments. The United States did not give support until the battleship *Maine* blew up in Havana harbor in 1898. Then the United States entered the war on the side of the Cuban rebels, with only six members of the House voting against the declaration of war.

The Spanish-American War indirectly caused Reed's exit from politics. He hated war and did not believe the Spanish were responsible for the *Maine* explosion. (Its cause has never been discovered.) As Speaker he could not vote on the war resolution, unless there was a tie, and he told one of the members who voted against it, "I envy you the luxury of your vote. I was where I could not do it." Reed thought the war could have been avoided and that McKinley had "the backbone of a chocolate éclair."[23]

Moreover, he was not in favor of annexing new territory to the U.S. or of adding overseas dependencies. Adding territory like Hawaii and the Philippines would be a source of weakness rather than strength, he believed.

Reed was in the minority, however. Embittered by the battle, he resigned from the speakership and from the House soon thereafter. At the end of the session on March 3, 1899, he retired and entered the private practice of law.

Reed left the House in stronger shape than it was when he entered it. Although he supported tariff and currency legislation in speeches, his greatest achievements were in parliamentary procedure. He was "the greatest parliamentary leader I ever saw," wrote his contemporary Henry Cabot Lodge.[24]

His success lay in removing the option of inaction. Those who thought government was inherently evil wanted a weak Speaker and barriers in the way of legislation. Reed had nothing but contempt for such a do-nothing policy. "We have got to do practical business in this House. Statesmanship does not consist in doing the best thing, but in doing the best possible thing. We have got to do what the resources of the country and, above all, what the sentiment of the country will support and sustain."[25]

Because of his sharp tongue and sarcastic wit, Reed was not as popular with his party as Clay had been with his. If dueling had still been in fashion, it was said, his tongue would surely have got him into trouble and his huge frame would have been too good a target to miss.[26] His own party passed him over for the presidential nomination in favor of a man with more popular appeal. Reed's intellectual power, however, and his determination to let the majority party rule accomplished what he may have lacked in other realms.

Reed left the speakership with the majority party firmly in control. His eventual successor, Joseph G. Cannon from Danville, Illinois, continued that tradition until he pushed it too far. Cannon would use all of Reed's Rules and more until a backlash against his power once more led to a dramatic confrontation with the Speaker in front of the dais.

|4|

JOE CANNON AND PROGRESS

"Everything is all right out West and around Danville. The country don't need any legislation."

Reed's Rules established the right of the majority party to govern, but what happens when the majority goes too far? The Speaker who came soon after Reed, Joseph Gurney Cannon, was also a firm believer in party politics. He was convinced it was the Speaker's duty to use all of the rules Reed had established and a few of his own to see that his party prevailed.

"I believe in consultin' the boys, findin' out what most of 'em want, and then goin' ahead and doin' it," Cannon avowed.[1] To his friends, he was "Uncle Joe." They were sure he and his fellow Republicans knew what was best for the country in the first decade of the twentieth century.

Others were not so sure. People in the United States were restless and uneasy over the intense economic and social developments of the previous century. To them Cannon was an obstacle to change—an obstacle to progress, some said. He wielded so much power that many members of the House felt they had no important part in making the laws. "For all practical purposes . . . our government is divided into three parts," said Representative George W. Norris of Nebraska, "the Senate, the

President, and the Speaker."[2] To his enemies, the Speaker was "Czar Cannon."

Joseph G. Cannon did not especially look like a boss. Cannon was as tall as Reed but "lean as a greyhound."[3] His alert blue-gray eyes sparkled from his narrow face, and his cheeks were ruddy. In one respect he did fit the image: a cigar dangled perpetually from the left side of his mouth as he talked out of the right. After forty years in Congress, ten thousand cigars had stained his white beard brown at the edges.

Cannon came from pioneer stock: a Quaker family that moved west from the South to Illinois to avoid living near slavery. When Joe was only fourteen, his father, a physician, died trying to cross a flooded stream to reach one of his sick patients. The boy went to work as a clerk in a country store to support his family, later studying and practicing law. Cannon saw himself as part of the "log-cabin, Abraham Lincoln" tradition although he had met the great Republican president only once.

Standing firm in that tradition, Cannon had no understanding of the mood of discontent in the country. America was experiencing the aftershocks of rapid industrialism, the type of growth Reed had supported with the protective tariff. As a result of that growth, free land in the West was rapidly disappearing and more people were living in cities. The urban population increased 34 percent from 1900 to 1910, much of it made up of immigrants from southern and eastern Europe. Divisions were appearing: between those who provided the capital for industry and those who provided the labor, between those who grew grain and those who shipped it, between those who lent money and those who borrowed.

In particular, farmers complained that the railroads set high rates for shipping their corn and wheat to market, rates they were powerless to change. They resented the huge profits the railroads were making by selling timber from the land the government had given them to build rails. Workers complained that wages were too low and hours too long, and that they had no control over their jobs. Women complained that although they might be working in factories alongside their children, they had no right to vote and that some alcoholic husbands drank up their wages rather than supporting their families. Conservationists complained that the government was selling forest and water rights so rapidly no resources would be left. Overall the discontented felt that the economically powerful were also politically powerful and were using that power to protect themselves at the expense of the public.

Senator Robert La Follette of Wisconsin stated it dramatically: "Democracy is on trial for its life in this country. A certain enemy is working against the wishes of the masses of the people which is described as a gathering together of those who are rich as against those who are not rich."[4]

The cure, reformers like La Follette thought, was to use the power of the federal government to intervene for the common good. States were too weak to control railroad shipping rates, for example, but the federal government could, through its constitutional power to regulate interstate commerce. The reformers espoused "a new idea": that the government is responsible for the well-being of all the people.

Cannon was deaf to these complaints. He contended that "America is a hell of a success," the greatest success in the world.[5] For forty years the country had prospered under a protective tariff. Why change it? He had grown up on a farm in Illinois when there was "no eight-hour law, no child labor law, no maternity law, and no compulsory school law," and he didn't see why any such laws were needed now. "Everything is all right out West and around Danville," he contended. "The country don't need any legislation."[6]

But everything was not all right out West. Representative Norris had been elected as a "regular" Republican from Nebraska, but he agreed with the complaints of his constituents and began to call himself a "progressive." For weeks he carried around in his pocket a resolution that would challenge the power of the Speaker, who he thought was an obstacle to progressive legislation. Norris waited patiently for the right moment to pull the resolution out of his pocket.

HAYSEED MEMBER FROM THE WILD AND WOOLY WEST

One reason Cannon felt confident of his position was that the Republicans had been the majority party for most of the previous fifty years. They were the party that had fought and won the Civil War and then consolidated the victory, the party of great men like Abraham Lincoln, Ulysses S. Grant, and General William T. Sherman. Democrats and various third parties like the Greenbacks and the Populists had so far been unable to challenge the Republican control.

As part of the dominant party, Cannon served in the House for fifty years, except for temporary defeats in 1890 and 1912. With his first speech in 1872 the House was treated to an eccentric style. When he became excited, Cannon's whole body expressed his feelings. He would beat the air with his left fist and prance jerkily along the aisles in a series of wild gestures. His left arm would pump up and down to accent each word while his right hand brushed at his wispy hair.[7]

Added to that style was a country label which Cannon encouraged. He asked in his first speech for a provision that would allow public documents to be sent through the mails free under the signature of a member of Congress. Seed, which Cannon and many other representatives sent to farmers, would also be allowed to be sent free, along with public documents. Cannon was interrupted by an

Eastern representative who observed he must have oats in his pockets.

"Yes . . . and hay-seed in my hair," Joe responded, evoking great laughter. From then on he was known as the Hayseed Member from the Wild and Woolly West, a reputation he preferred to being known merely as an "also spoke."[8]

Hayseed or not, he won an appointment to the Rules Committee in 1883 as a minority member, and then Reed appointed him again in 1889 as a majority member. Cannon was also chairman of the Appropriations Committee, "the Watchdog of the Treasury," in four Congresses.

"You think it is my business to make appropriations," Cannon observed, "but it is not. It is to prevent their being made."[9]

One appropriation he did support, despite Reed's opposition, was $50 million to prepare for war after the *Maine* exploded in Havana Harbor. When Reed retired over his disagreement with the expansionist sentiments of the time, he was succeeded for four years by George Henderson of Iowa and then by Cannon in 1904.

UNCLE JOE AS SPEAKER

Cannon was not an outstanding legislator. During the half century he served in the House, no piece of legislation bore his name as its author. Instead he came to power as a party man. His own authority depended on the support of Republicans. Moreover, he believed that party rule was superior to one-man rule. Idols, he observed, have feet of clay.

Uncle Joe was no idol; his coarse language belied that label, but those who knew him liked him. His leadership style was much more personal than Reed's. He preferred to transact business at private get-togethers over a few drinks and between poker hands. After he turned sixty (in 1896) Cannon decided to skip lunch every day in the

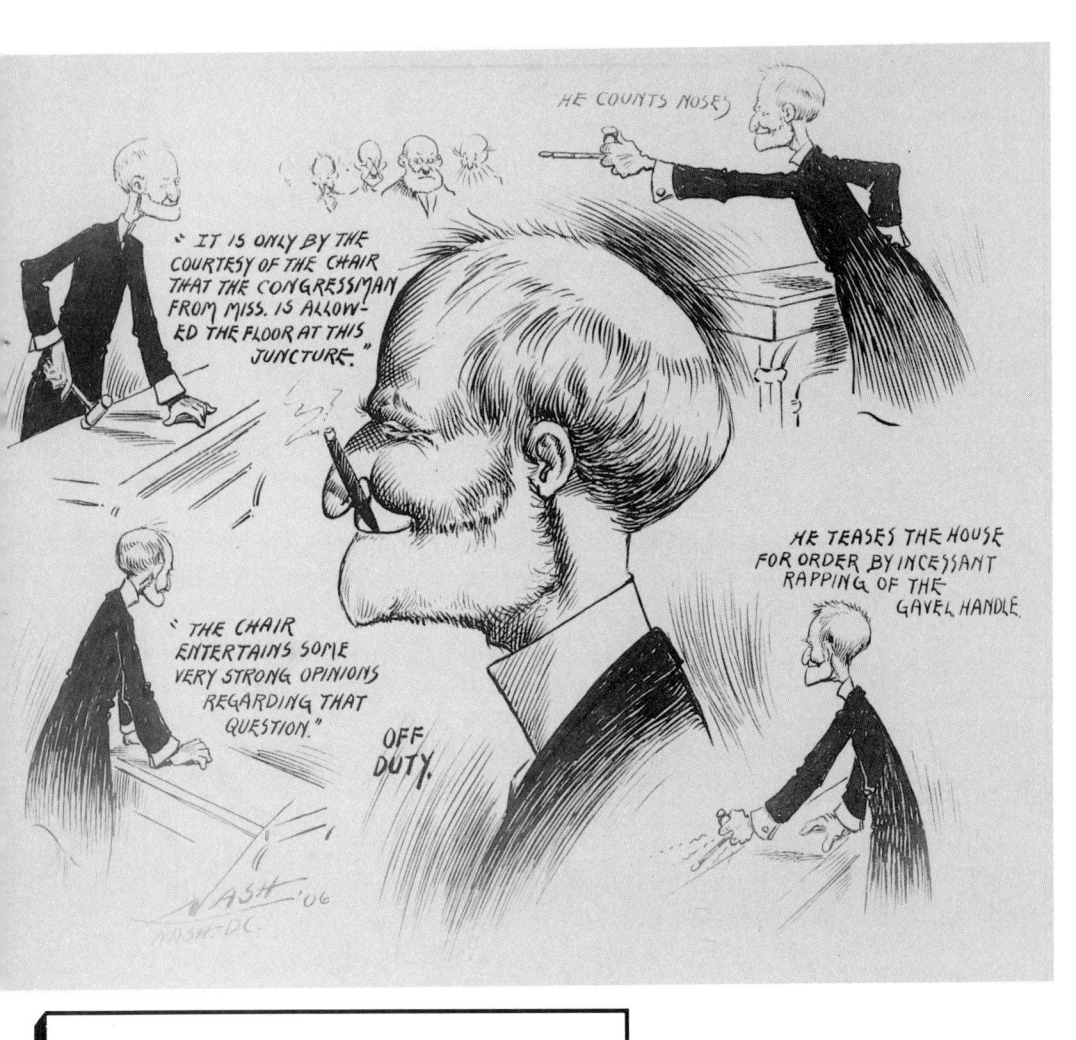

This 1906 cartoon lampoons Joseph Cannon's eccentric style as Speaker of the House, and features the characteristic cigar that always hung from the left side of his mouth.

belief that that would prolong his life, but he still went along to lunch with his cronies because he enjoyed their company. Those who supported him received the favor of a committee chairmanship and the office that went with it. Those who crossed him were punished.

"It's a damned good thing to remember in politics," he proclaimed, "to stick to your party and never attempt to buy the favor of your enemies at the expense of your friends."[10]

From poker came the term most often used to describe Cannon. A player who declines to discard cards and draw new (and possibly better) ones after the deal is called a standpatter. Cannon was unwilling to pass laws or make changes in the hope that things would be better; he preferred to stand pat. In his estimation, half of the proposals for reform were harmful and the rest were useless.

By standing pat against the reformers, Uncle Joe became the defender of the status quo. Those benefiting from the status quo were the big businesses, monopolies, and corporations. That was fine with Cannon. Business, he believed, "has been the inspiration behind all our marvellous achievement." Even for the pioneers, he said, the lure was "profit, always profit," and he saw nothing wrong with that.[11]

Similarly, he believed opportunity would come to every individual who was self-reliant: "Let every tub stand on its own bottom."[12] Like the mostly small-town Midwesterners who supported him, Cannon wanted to continue the kind of America in which they had flourished.

Although his stonewalling benefited the corporations, Uncle Joe helped them because of his own convictions, not because he was corrupt. No one accused him of taking bribes from the economic giants as other politicians had done.

George Norris, however, figured the status quo was

harmful. The muckrakers were arousing public opinion. Journalists like Upton Sinclair had poked into the working and sanitary conditions in Chicago's huge meat-packing plants and found them abysmal. No less powerful a figure than Theodore Roosevelt had come into the presidency in 1901 talking reform. Even though he came from a wealthy family himself, Roosevelt thought the very rich had prospered at the expense of the common people. He did not like the social conditions he saw or the criticism he was hearing.

TR thought the Interstate Commerce Commission (ICC) should fix railroad rates. The tariff should be revised so as not to protect large businesses that didn't need it. He wanted to conserve the nation's forests. He even considered an income tax, an inheritance tax, federal investigation of labor disputes, and laws to govern the employment of women and children.

To secure these changes, however, Roosevelt had to deal with Cannon, and Cannon would not be moved. He opposed the taxes; he didn't want to give the federal government any more power than it had; besides, it didn't need any more money. Conservation? "Not one damn cent for scenery." Roosevelt did secure one cherished piece of legislation: giving the ICC full power to fix railroad rates. Most of the time, however, Cannon's opinion on legislation prevailed, and Roosevelt's program went nowhere.

Progressive voices had been raised in the Senate, too. Robert La Follette of Wisconsin, elected to the House in 1884, governor of Wisconsin for three terms, then to the Senate in 1906, represented the farmers' interests against the railroads. Through fiery rhetoric he became the chief spokesman for reform and unifier of the progressives. Progressive measures had to pass both the Senate and the House, however, where La Follette's stubbornness confronted Cannon's.

Sam Gompers, too, had come up against Cannon.

Samuel Gompers, the president of the American Federation of Labor, battled with Congress to have laws passed restricting the use of injunctions against striking labor unions.

Gompers was the president of the new American Federation of Labor, the national organization of labor unions. Unions were young and had only a few methods by which to push their demands for higher wages and an eight-hour day. Their main tool was the strike, but the courts had not allowed long strikes, issuing injunctions to stop them. What Gompers wanted from Congress were laws restricting the use of injunctions and exempting labor unions from prosecution for interfering with trade when they boycotted a dealer.

In the spirit of each tub standing on its own bottom, Cannon thought labor's ideas were ridiculous. An employer had every right to fire a worker for any reason, he said, including belonging to a union. Pioneers in Illinois hadn't needed someone to regulate their working day, and he didn"t think urban workers needed it either.

There were other battles over specific laws: a literacy test for immigrants, prohibition bills, meat inspection and pure-foods laws, women's suffrage, a tariff on newsprint. Whenever an issue Cannon opposed threatened to enter the legislative debate, he drew on the many tools a Speaker had to stymie legislation. He refused to recognize members he did not want to hear. Unless they had told him in advance what they planned to say, he ignored them. He controlled floor debate by using the Rules Committee to keep bills from being considered by the full House. During each session he stated on his own what bills would pass and which ones would fail. Asked once if a certain bill had a chance of passing, he responded, "This House could pass an elephant if the gentleman in charge of it could catch the Speaker's eye." [13]

He made no pretense of impartiality. He was not one of those Speakers, he said, whom reformers expected "to be nothing more than a Sunday School teacher, to pat all the good little boys on the head and turn the other cheek when the bad boys use him as a target for their bean shooters."

Once, after a voice vote, he admitted, "The ayes make the most noise, but the nays have it." Counting a "rising vote" with the delegates on their feet, he began, "One, two, three, four—oh, hell, a hundred."[14]

Moreover, he used committee assignments to reward and punish lawmakers who supported or crossed him. The House had sixty-two standing committees at the turn of the century, and the sixty-two chairmen were the only lawmakers with private offices, free stationery, and an extra $125 a month to hire a clerk. In addition to these perks, a committee chairman had a much better chance of seeing his bills pass. The Speaker appointed the committee members and the chairman, whom he could also remove at will, regardless of seniority.

OPPOSITION TO CZAR CANNON

As long as Cannon and the regular Republicans represented the majority of the public, he could get away with acting like a czar. George Norris began carrying a resolution around in his pocket because he thought Cannon no longer represented the majority. Instead he was using "the power of his high position to prevent the consideration of legislation asked for by the people and desired by a large body of the members of the House of Representatives."

Indeed, by the campaign of 1908, Cannon himself was an issue. Democrats and some Republicans said he was the absolute tyrant of the House. From the security of the Senate, La Follette said bluntly: "It is my hope and my prayer that Joe Cannon will be defeated. . . . The voice of the people is strangled and stifled by this man. There is a tyranny there that makes men cringe and crawl, that makes cowards of the Republicans of the House."[15]

Nevertheless, Cannon, presidential candidate William H. Taft, and the Republicans won again in 1908.

The Democrats gained 10 seats in the House for a total of 173, but the Republicans still had a strong majority at 218. At least 24 of those Republicans, however, were anti-Cannon. They became known as Insurgents.

When the 61st Congress convened on March 15, 1909, once again the Republicans elected Cannon Speaker, but Democrat Champ Clark introduced a motion to increase the size of the Rules Committee from five to fifteen and have the members elected by the House instead of appointed by the Speaker. Responding adroitly to this challenge, Cannon wooed some Democrats to his side, some from New York who didn't want to see the federal excise tax on beer go up, and some from the South who wanted to protect lumber in their states with a tariff.

Cannon won that vote, but one rule change was made. On Wednesdays, members would no longer have to get the Speaker's permission to bring up a bill for discussion. On "Calendar Wednesday" any bill could be considered and a two-thirds majority of the House would be required to override the calendar.

Cannon didn't much like Calendar Wednesday, but it had little effect on the main issue of the 1909 session, tariffs. In their campaign, Republicans had promised to revise tariffs downward, easing some of the protection businesses had enjoyed for so long. Taft wanted to keep that promise, and a weak tariff bill did pass the House, revising the Dingley Tariff set in 1887. The Senate, however, added 847 amendments. More than half of them were increases instead of decreases, many catering to special interests like the woolen and cotton industries of New England.

That was fine with Cannon. He made sure he appointed House members who were committed to high tariffs to the conference committee assigned to work out the differences between the House and Senate versions of the bill. In the resulting law 4,000 items were included, but tariffs were reduced on only 400. Taft realized too late what was happening to the legislation. By then, Cannon refused to compromise. The resulting Payne-Aldrich Tariff was an embarrassment to the Republicans, and the public felt betrayed.

The time was right for Norris's resolution.

CHALLENGE TO THE SPEAKER

His first opportunity came in a debate over a favorite progressive issue: conservation. Americans were gradually becoming aware that private companies were using up the country's greatest natural resources for profit. Gifford Pinchot, chief forester of the United States and genius of the conservation movement, warned that Americans would bequeath a poverty-stricken country to their children and grandchildren if they exhausted the forests and other natural resources. The biggest battles came over water and timber.

In 1891 Congress had passed the Forest Reserve Act, which allowed the president to set aside forests in the Far West for public, not private, use. When Cannon was Speaker, nine other bills were introduced to establish forest reserves in the White Mountains and southern Appalachians, but Cannon deflected the bills by referring them to the Judiciary Committee instead of to the more sympathetic Agriculture Committee. When the governors created a Conservation Commission in 1908, Cannon prevented it from functioning by forbidding any government division to lend its employees to the commission.

The conservation issue came to a head in a dispute over the sale of public lands containing water power sites in Wyoming and Montana. Under President Theodore Roosevelt, the secretary of the interior had removed those sites from the lands electric power companies could purchase, but under President Taft, Secretary of the

Chief Forester Gifford Pinchot feared that the United States would exhaust its natural resources if bills protecting public lands were not passed.

Interior Richard A. Ballinger put them back up for sale. Pinchot protested and charged Ballinger with favoritism toward companies he had represented as a lawyer. When Pinchot made his protests public, Taft fired him. Congress decided to investigate.

Pinchot and Cannon had always disagreed. "From my point of view Uncle Joe was usually wrong," wrote Pinchot in his autobiography.[16] The Insurgents wanted to stand behind Pinchot in the investigation, but Cannon was expected to back Ballinger and produce a whitewash from the investigation. The Insurgents had one big obstacle to overcome: Cannon would appoint the House members of the investigating committee.

Norris had been observing the Speaker's habits. He knew that John Dalzell, a Republican regular from Pennsylvania, often filled in for the Speaker and that every day at 1:00 P.M. Dalzell headed for a sandwich, cup of coffee, and piece of pie at the House restaurant. On January 19, 1910, Dalzell left for lunch as usual and gave the gavel to Walter I. Smith. Norris approached Smith who agreed to give him five minutes on the floor, suspecting nothing unusual.

The representative from Nebraska kept his Rules Committee resolution in his pocket for the moment. This time he offered an amendment to let the House appoint the members of the investigating committee. The amendment passed by three votes.

This small success infuriated Cannon and emboldened the Insurgents. Two months later, on a Calendar Wednesday, Cannon inadvertently gave Norris a bigger opening. In a procedural ruling, the Speaker said that a census-related bill was privileged under the Constitution and could interrupt the normal business of the House. Cannon made the ruling because he disliked Calendar Wednesday, when any bill could be discussed; he was happy to allow the census bill to interrupt the day. His ruling was appealed, however, and overturned.

The next day, Thursday, March 17, many Republican members were absent, celebrating St. Patrick's Day and the long weekend to come. The persistent sponsor of the census bill brought it up again. Cannon repeated his ruling that the bill was privileged under the Constitution and could be called up at any time.

While the roll call vote on Cannon's ruling was counted, Norris pulled from his pocket a piece of paper that had become so tattered and worn it scarcely hung together. Quickly he copied the resolution, which he knew by heart, on the front and back of an old envelope. At the end of the roll call, which upheld the Speaker's ruling, he jumped to his feet, waved the envelope in the air, and declared, "Mr. Speaker, I present a resolution made privileged by the Constitution."

Unaware of what was to come, Cannon allowed the envelope to be submitted to the clerk and read. The resolution proposed to reduce the power of the Rules Committee by enlarging it to fifteen members, each representing a geographical area. More significantly, the members would be elected by the House, rather than appointed by the Speaker, and the Speaker would be ineligible for membership. The resolution was privileged under the Constitution, Norris claimed, because Article I, Section 5, Paragraph 2 of the Constitution says, "Each House may determine the rules of its proceedings."[17]

CANNON REPLIES

The House sat in stunned silence for a moment as Cannon looked on. Then a point of order was raised, and the House waited to see whether Cannon would dare to rule Norris's resolution out of order. Cannon delayed ruling and quickly sent out word to Republican regulars to rush back to Washington. "The fight began at once and it will go down into the history of the House as one of the most stubborn partisan struggles ever witnessed in that body," said the *New York Sun*.

Standpatters began a filibuster, waiting for Cannon to gather the loyalists. The Insurgents refused to allow a recess, hoping to wear out the regulars, and crowds flocked to the galleries when they heard the Speaker's power had been challenged. As the speeches droned on late into the night and early morning, the New York *Evening Post* reported that "All pretense of the politeness that normally rules proceedings in the House was thrown aside."[18]

Cannon spent the night sleeping on a red couch in the Speaker's rooms near the House chamber, but he was often interrupted by conferences, telephoning, and telegraphing to the absentees. He returned to the chair early in the morning, then went out for breakfast. As the members grew more snappish, the Democrats agreed to a recess at 10:00 A.M. for the purpose of trying to reach a compromise. The compromise efforts stalled, however, on the issue of excluding the Speaker from the Rules Committee; Cannon would not give in on that point.

Finally it was apparent that Cannon would not be able to rally enough regulars to return to the Capitol and support him. At 4:00 P.M., as the House reconvened, he announced that he was prepared to make a ruling on the point of order. With a ruling promised, the House recessed until Saturday morning, March 19.

Dressed in fresh clothes his servant had brought to the Capitol, Cannon calmly ruled that, unlike the census resolution, Norris's resolution was not in order. He said the proposal "would overturn the rule of the majority, which is the principle upon which democracy must rest."[19] Norris immediately jumped to his feet and appealed the ruling. On a dramatic vote, the Speaker—and his opposition to progress—were voted down, 182 to 163.

Norris next amended his resolution to provide for ten

Rules Committee members elected by the House, six of the majority party and four of the minority. The Speaker would not be a member, and the committee would select its own chair; the geographical feature was eliminated. His amended proposal was then approved, 191 to 156, with forty-two Republicans voting for it.

Although he had been overruled and his power diminished, Cannon was not yet out. He told the representatives there were two choices: he could resign and let them choose a new Speaker, or they could declare a vacancy in the office of Speaker and elect a new one. He would not resign, he said, because that would be a "confession of weakness or mistake of [sic] an apology for past actions. The Speaker is not conscious of having done any political wrong."[20]

He then left the floor, accompanied by applause. A motion to declare the speakership vacant did not pass. Cannon would remain as Speaker but with much less power. No longer would his word and his will be enough to stop legislation the majority wanted.

PROGRESSIVE TRIUMPH

Cannon was still an issue in the elections of 1910 because he refused to say he wouldn't run for Speaker again. Subsequently, the Democrats won control of the House for the first time in sixteen years. Champ Clark became Speaker and Cannon an ordinary representative.

Two years later, the Republican party split, with Theodore Roosevelt running as a Progressive candidate and Taft running for reelection as a Republican. Cannon feared that "the uplift magazines and the college professors" would take over.[21] Sure enough, one of the latter did. Democrat and college professor Woodrow Wilson was elected president, and Cannon was defeated in his own district.

Soon thereafter the country was flooded with progres-

With the 1912 split between the Republican and Progressive parties, Joe Cannon feared an onslaught of liberal legislation. His worst fears were realized with the election of Woodrow Wilson, a Democrat from New Jersey.

sive legislation, including an income tax amendment to the Constitution, a prohibition amendment, the designation of national forests, the Federal Reserve Act creating central control over banking and currency, a downward revision of the tariff, and the establishment of the Federal Trade Commission. The Cannon dam was broken.

Cannon was reelected in 1914 and continued in Congress until 1922. He never changed his mind about the rightness of what he had done as Speaker. When he retired at the age of eighty-six he still didn't see any reason for being dissatisfied with American life. "I think I can honestly say that the nation is the strongest in the world, and the people are growing better and better every day."[22]

Yet his worldview had been superseded by the new idea, expressed by Teddy Roosevelt when he returned from lion hunting in Africa: "The man who wrongly holds that every human right is secondary to his profit must now give way to the advocate of human welfare, who rightly maintains that every man holds his property subject to the general right of the community to regulate its use to whatever degree the public welfare may require it."[23]

Although Cannon's ideas were defeated, his real legacy was the example of using his party's power and the position of Speaker to further strong convictions. A later Speaker, William Bankhead, said of both Reed and Cannon that no matter whether one agreed with their views, "We must necessarily admire the grip they had on their parties and their firm determination to rule this House in large measure according to their view of their public and party duties."[24] Later speakers could never match the dictatorial power Uncle Joe had wielded. They would find new ways to secure the support of the majority.

|5|

SAM RAYBURN AND CIVIL RIGHTS

"To get along, a person sometimes has to go along."

I n 1913, the year Joe Cannon was defeated, young Sam Rayburn came to Congress from the low hills and prairies of northeastern Texas. Rayburn was barely thirty-one, only slightly older than Henry Clay had been when he joined the House, but Rayburn would stay for the rest of his life. Seventeen of those years he would be Speaker, twice as long as Clay.

On that brisk March day after his own election, Rayburn had come to Washington early to see Woodrow Wilson inaugurated as president. The same Progressive movement that toppled Cannon had split the Republicans and opened the way for a Democratic triumph. Wilson was the first Democratic president in sixteen years, and Rayburn was thrilled.

Listening in the cold, Sam Rayburn heard the new president promise a "new freedom" to the American people. They would lead better and richer lives, Wilson said, as the powers of big business were reduced. This promise appealed to the Texan, who knew the importance of opportunity for the ordinary person. He had just missed becoming a tenant farmer himself, he said, by "a gnat's whisker."[1]

Born in 1882 in a log cabin in Tennessee, the eighth

of eleven children, Sam soon moved with his family to a farm in Texas. On the desolate and sparsely settled land, there was little for a boy to do but work, fourteen to sixteen hours a day.

"On Sunday I used to sit on the fence in front of the house and wish and wish and wish that somebody would ride by on a horse or in a buggy—just anybody to relieve the monotony, just somebody to see and wave at," Rayburn remembered.[2]

One rainy Saturday when Sam was twelve or thirteen, he was allowed to ride the mule twelve miles from the community of Flag Springs into the town of Bonham, the county seat, to hear his district's congressman, Joseph Weldon Bailey. Sam was too shy to go into the large tent with the townsfolk, but he found an open flap and listened for two hours as the rain dripped down his neck. Then he followed the tall, handsome Bailey several blocks through town. At home that night he announced to his brothers and sisters that Sam Rayburn himself would go to Congress someday.

First he wanted to attend college, so he saved five dollars, enough for the railroad fare to Mayo Normal College in a nearby town. His father gave him twenty dollars more, and at Mayo, Sam got a job as a janitor and bell ringer. When that wasn't enough, he dropped out for a year to teach and earn his tuition. After he graduated in 1903, Rayburn taught school for three more years, but his true calling was politics. In 1906 he ran for the Texas House of Representatives. He served there for three terms and was elected Speaker at age twenty-nine.

Sam had never lost sight of his boyhood goal. In 1912 he announced he was running for Congress, and he won the Democratic nomination over seven other opponents. That guaranteed him the election. The persistence and honesty of this college-educated farmer earned him the loyalty of Fourth District voters. They never voted him out in forty-eight years.

Sam Rayburn served in Congress for forty-eight years, and before his seventeen-year tenure as Speaker of the House, he worked on various committees. During his long career, he helped bring together representatives who had divergent viewpoints to pass important civil rights laws.

A SOUTHERN RURAL DEMOCRAT

As the 62nd Congress began, the House had reached its full size of 435 members. The individual desks were removed and replaced with unassigned seats. Rayburn and everyone else could choose whatever seat was available.

Choosing his course in the House was more difficult, but the newcomer was lucky to receive some advice from a fellow Texan, John Nance Garner. Garner had already been there for ten years. He said that the two most powerful committees were Ways and Means, which Garner had his eye on, and the Interstate and Foreign Commerce Committee. Garner's close friend was chairman of Interstate and Foreign Commerce; Rayburn was soon appointed a member.

As it had for Clay, Rayburn's political education continued in the evenings, this time in the lobby of the Cochran Hotel, where he and other members of Congress were staying. "Each night after supper," he recalled, "most of these men would pull their chairs together at the end of the big old lobby. For several hours they would explore together the great issues of the hour."

What were those issues, and what did Sam Rayburn believe in? Wilson was the first president since John Adams to address the House in person at the beginning of the session. He laid out a full legislative program: a reduction in the tariff to promote free trade with the rest of the world; a federal reserve system to provide help for banks in an emergency; new antitrust laws; and aid to farmers and workers.

Rayburn especially liked the lower tariff (which would lower the price of farm equipment), education for farm boys and girls, and measures making it easier for farmers to get loans. He also supported an income tax, an inheritance tax, labor's right to organize, and the direct election of senators instead of election by legislatures.

Despite the support of Democrats like Rayburn, Wilson's program was sidetracked by World War I. Then came three Republican presidents and a stretch of Republican majorities. When the Democrats regained a majority in 1931, Jack Garner was named Speaker. Rayburn's own influence increased when he was named chair of the Interstate and Foreign Commerce Committee.

By the time he became a committee chair, Rayburn was nearly bald. That shining dome became a trademark atop his solid five-foot, six-inch frame. At age forty-nine, Rayburn was also a bachelor. He had married in 1927, but the marriage lasted only three months. Rayburn never said much about it to anyone. He typically kept his personal life to himself.

As Rayburn acquired more power in the House, the Great Depression was growing in force. Its effects were obvious in his district. Banks were closed, farms were sold, town businesses went bankrupt, and auctions of a family's goods or a business's assets were frequent. Rayburn thought government should do something.

At the 1932 Democratic convention, he supported his friend Garner for the presidential nomination, but Franklin D. Roosevelt was nominated and elected that fall with Garner as vice president. In his first 100 days as president, Roosevelt immediately asked Congress for New Deal legislation to attack the causes and effects of the Depression.

Rayburn used his committee chairmanship to give Roosevelt much of what he asked for. His committee reported the Securities Act of 1933, a law regulating railroad holding companies. It also passed measures creating the Securities and Exchange Commission and the Federal Communications Commission.

Throughout his political career, Rayburn always voted for what he thought was fair and reasonable, which was usually somewhere in the mainstream of Democratic thought. However, he was not afraid to pull ahead on

After the Stock Market Crash in 1929, several banks failed and many businesses went bankrupt, leading to massive unemployment and poverty.

some issues, such as control of utilities. After a fierce battle, his committee reported and Congress passed the Utility Holding Company Act, which reduced the influence of the few men who ran the giant utility companies Probably his most satisfying work was passage of the 1936 Rural Electrification Administration Act, which brought lights to isolated rural areas like Flag Springs.

With such substantial accomplishments, Rayburn moved up to majority leader in 1937, right before his fifty-fifth birthday. For the first of many times, Rayburn learned how hard it could be to hold the Democrats together, despite their large majority. Three years later, however, when Speaker William B. Bankhead died, Rayburn had earned enough admiration and respect that his colleagues elected him Speaker.

REASONABLE PERSUASION

Rayburn became Speaker at a crucial time. In 1941 German armies were marching through Europe to the east as the United States tried to remain neutral. Preparing for what seemed inevitable, Congress had initiated a draft, selecting 600,000 men into the Army for one year in September 1940. Parents of the draftees and opponents of U.S. entry into World War II were calling for the men's release at the end of their first year. All of Rayburn's experience in the House would be tested in his first major struggle as Speaker.

Rayburn favored extension of the draft in order to support the president and prepare for war. Just four months before the Japanese attack on Pearl Harbor, the new Speaker went from representative to representative making one-on-one appeals: "Do this for me. I won't forget it."[4] After a bitter three-day floor fight and a tense roll call, Rayburn read the slip of paper handed to him by the clerk. Without expression he announced that the ayes were 203 and the noes 202. Moving quickly, he

Sam Rayburn faced his first struggle in the House in the summer of 1941, when Congress, in preparation for the United States' entry into World War II, extended the draft.

headed off any motion for reconsideration of the vote, gaveled down hard, and declared the bill had passed.

Rayburn's characteristic single loud crack of the gavel and his command of parliamentary procedure were only part of his style as Speaker. In this first tangle, he had also proved he could get the votes when he needed them with a process he called reasonable persuasion. "The old day of pounding on the desk and giving people hell is gone," Rayburn claimed. "A man's got to lead by persuasion and kindness and the best reason—that's the only way he can lead people."[5] Over the years Rayburn perfected the art of reasonable persuasion and applied it to hundreds of representatives. His sense of what was reasonable and his ability to persuade were tested time and again on the great domestic issue of the 1950s, civil rights.

"POVERTY ... IS VERY DANGEROUS"

Roosevelt died in office in 1945, and Vice President Harry Truman of Missouri succeeded him. Both Rayburn and Truman were Southerners, practical, straightforward, plain-spoken politicians. Truman agreed with Rayburn's advice that if you tell people the truth the first time "you don't have any trouble remembering what you said."[6]

Truman was ahead of Rayburn on civil rights, however. Lynchings of blacks in the South, segregation in the armed forces, discrimination in employment came to the fore during and after the war. By executive order Roosevelt had established a Fair Employment Practices Commission to prevent racial discrimination in war-industry hiring, but Southerners in Congress cut its funding at the end of the war. Then Truman appointed a committee to survey the state of civil rights in the nation. The committee's report, "To Secure These Rights," was blunt: widespread discrimination was a basic fact of life in the United States.

In response, Truman ordered an end to all discrimination in the armed forces and federal civil service. Early in 1948, an election year, he also called Rayburn to his office. Republicans had a majority in the House, and Rayburn was the minority leader. Nevertheless, the president handed him an ambitious civil rights bill that included an end to Jim Crow laws (segregated seating) in interstate transportation, elimination of the poll tax (a financial restriction on voting), a federal antilynching law, and continuation of the FEPC. Rayburn took the bill but said nothing.

Mr. Sam (as Texans called him) and his district were both conservative on issues of race. In the 1940s he supported segregation in public accommodations and in schools. He was wary of federal intervention in racial matters, even federal aid to education, and he repeatedly voted against national antilynching bills. He thought blacks were inferior, and he feared intermarriage.

Yet Rayburn had considerable compassion for the poverty he saw: "I always feel a little blue when I see some of the dilapidated houses and dire circumstances in which too many of our colored folk have to live," he said. "Poverty is not only a sad thing to see, but I think it is very dangerous. Extreme destitution can defile any society."[7]

Back in his office, Rayburn stashed Truman's civil rights bill in a lower desk drawer. He decided to support the president's public housing program but not civil rights. Even if it made humanitarian sense, he thought the bill would be too controversial in an election year. He did not think the South was ready to eliminate segregation and shouldn't be pushed into it.

Southern politicians were incensed by the mere announcement of Truman's program. Rayburn tried to calm their fears and warned that the South could not filibuster forever. Besides his dislike of poverty, Rayburn would also defend anyone's right to vote. He urged the Texas governor to abolish the state poll tax, which was used to keep blacks from voting. Southerners "must give the Negroes a better break if they want to prevent passage of Federal civil rights legislation such as the FEPC," he told them.[8]

In both the House and in the presidential nominating convention that summer Rayburn had the difficult job of holding the fractious Democrats together. In the House Rayburn postponed action on controversial legislation like civil rights but quietly moved along progressive legislation he thought was not too far ahead of its time. At the convention, as presiding officer, he tried to prevent the Southern Democrats from bolting because he thought it would devastate the party and ruin Truman's chances. Northern liberals like Hubert Humphrey succeeded, however, in getting a strong civil rights plank into the platform.

Rayburn knew that when the platform came up for a vote, Alabama planned to lead a walkout as soon as the state was called at the beginning of the roll call. Thinking ahead to forestall that, Rayburn asked for a voice vote on the platform instead. He declared that the "ayes" had it. Choosing not to follow up with a roll call, Rayburn quickly recessed the convention to the loud boos of the Southerners.

Rayburn's tactic succeeded. Thirty-five "Dixiecrats" did stomp out of the convention the next day, but that was far fewer than would have left the day before. In the election that fall, four Southern states supported South Carolina governor Strom Thurmond for president, but Truman was narrowly elected over the Republican candidate, Thomas Dewey. After two years of Republican control, Democrats regained a majority in the House, and

Rayburn was Speaker once again. The credit or blame for legislating on civil rights would go to the Democrats. Rayburn approached the issue with great caution.

GOING ALONG

Despite their majority, the tension between the Northern liberals and Southern conservatives threatened the Democrats' fragile unity. When Congress convened, some Democrats urged that the Dixiecrats be punished for abandoning the presidential candidate. Typically avoiding confrontation, Rayburn looked for a way to mollify the liberals without losing the conservatives. He supported a new twenty-one-day rule intended to pry progressive legislation out of the conservative Rules Committee.

The Rules Committee was the traffic cop of the House. It could hurry a bill through or slow it down. It could refuse to schedule hearings on a bill or refuse to grant a rule under which the bill could be debated on the floor. When House members really didn't want to vote on a controversial issue, the Rules Committee could hold on to it and protect members from their constituents' wrath. As it was constituted in 1949, however, the committee was more of a roadblock than a buffer. Two Southern Democrats usually voted with the four Republican members, resulting in 6–6 ties, which kept liberal legislation from the floor.

Under the rule Rayburn supported, if the Rules Committee kept a bill that had been reported by another committee for more than twenty-one days, the chairman of that committee could bring the bill before the House. Rayburn was not entirely in favor of freeing liberal bills from the Rules Committee's clutches, but the rule also gave him more power to control the flow of legislation. When it passed, he told committee chairs they would have to clear bills they wanted to call up with him.

Right away Rayburn used that prerogative to stall civil rights. When Education and Labor Committee Chairman John Lesinski tried to spring Truman's FEPC bill from the Rules Committee, Rayburn refused to recognize him.

Rayburn had no compunction about using the formal power of his position. "The Speaker should be a man of strength," he said. "Naturally any strong leader will use all the power that is given him or he can get."[9] More than formal power, however, he relied on personal influence, the carrot rather than the stick. Rayburn believed that the people would come around to a reasonable position if issues were explained in the right way.

Talking to some of his constituents at home about the need for an agriculture program and how it would help the standard of living throughout the country, he made an oft-quoted statement: "The good people will go along with such a program, I believe. You know, in order to get along, a person sometimes has to go along. That does not imply that anybody ever has to become a rubber stamp because when two minds always agree, one of them is doing all the thinking. But where there is an umpire in the game and a ruling is made, I learned in baseball that it is a poor player who becomes angry, throws his bat at the umpire, and quits the game like a spoiled child."[10]

Going along to get along was the oil that moved the House. If the oil wasn't there yet on an issue, Rayburn could be patient.

Discouraged by a long and bitter session in 1950 and by Southern filibusters, Truman gave up on civil rights legislation. Nevertheless, he had brought the issue into the legislative debate. In his farewell address in 1952 he cited an "awakening of the American conscience."[11] The "good people" would soon be willing to go along. The next sessions forced hard decisions on the Supreme Court, on the president, and on the Speaker.

President Harry Truman gave up on civil rights legislation, but in his farewell address, he confidently predicted an "awakening of the American conscience."

EISENHOWER'S TURN

Lawsuits asserting equal rights had been working their long, slow way through the court system. After seventeen years of litigation, whites-only primaries were found unconstitutional in 1944. In 1954, the Supreme Court decided in *Brown* v. *Board of Education of Topeka, Kansas,* that separate schools for black and white children provided unequal educations. They were thus a violation of the Fourteenth Amendment to the Constitution, which provides for equal protection of the laws to all citizens.

That landmark decision aroused passions in the South and raised questions across the nation. Would the decision lead to federal intervention to secure school desegregation and other rights, as the South feared? Rayburn still favored school segregation, but he accepted the Court's authority. He only hoped the Court would give the South enough time to change. Late in 1955, however, the U.S. attorney general, Herbert Brownell, began drafting a broad civil rights program that President Dwight Eisenhower could present to Congress.

Sam Rayburn understood the political dilemma in civil rights legislation. Both Republicans and Democrats knew that support from Northern industrial cities was important in electing presidents, and the cities supported civil rights. Southern Democrats did not, and yet they were important to the party if the Democrats wanted to maintain a majority in Congress. If Rayburn supported the legislation, he risked splitting his own party. If he did not, Democrats risked losing the 1956 election.

Republicans did not face the same conflict, but President Eisenhower did not have great enthusiasm for a civil rights bill, either. He did not approve Brownell's program until April of 1956, which was a late date to introduce major legislation in an election year.

The bill contained several provisions. The first established a bipartisan Civil Rights Commission to look into charges that blacks were not permitted to vote and were threatened with job losses if they tried. A second established a new assistant attorney general in the Justice Department to bring action when civil rights were violated. Other parts of the bill contained stronger enforcement of voting rights and provisions to allow the federal government to take civil as well as criminal action to enforce civil rights.

Once the legislation was introduced, a tug-of-war began. Northern liberals wanted to be able to vote for a civil rights bill before the fall elections. Southern conservatives wanted to avoid such a vote. One hundred Southern senators and representatives had signed a Southern Manifesto in March denouncing "outside agitators" who were threatening "revolutionary changes" in the public school system.[12]

The man who had introduced the manifesto and the leader of the conservatives was Howard W. Smith of Virginia, chairman of the Rules Committee. Smith was a veteran in manipulating House rules in his favor; his power rivaled the Speaker's. He knew the bill would pass if it came to a floor vote. He also knew he could not delay the vote indefinitely. However, if he could delay it until the end of the session in July, the Senate would not act in time to pass a law that year.

Rayburn could help or hurt the bill's passage. Richard Bolling of Missouri, a strong supporter of voting rights legislation, had talked to the Speaker about such legislation in January. That spring Rayburn was still wary of forcing civil rights on the South, but on voting rights he was leaning toward change. After listening patiently to Bolling's explanation, Rayburn commented tersely, "I'm not against the right to vote. Every citizen should have that."[13] From that brief statement, Bolling concluded that the Speaker would step in at the right time.

Rayburn would know when his support was needed. He could read the mood of the House, it was said, "as

Pictured from left to right are George Hayes, Thurgood Marshall, and James Nabrit, Jr., the lawyers who argued against segregation in the landmark Brown v. Board of Education *case. With the Supreme Court's 1954 decision, Sam Rayburn was faced with a new dilemma in civil rights legislation.*

other men read their morning newspapers."[14] From the moment he walked into the hall at the beginning of the day's session, he knew whether it was a good day for passing legislation or a day for waiting for controversy to settle.

To obtain that feel, Rayburn kept his office door open. "Let me know if you hear anything" was his favorite conversation closer. In the evenings, in a small room "downstairs" in the Capitol, he would meet with old and trusted friends to plot strategy or exchange news about bills.

"The Speaker has to be utterly responsive to the waves of sentiment rolling out from [the House's] members," Rayburn maintained. "If he does not have the feel of the House, he is lost and he might as well quit."[15]

THE 1956 CIVIL RIGHTS BILL

Eisenhower's bill was introduced and referred to the House Judiciary Committee, whose chairman, Emanuel Celler of Brooklyn, was a strong supporter of civil rights. He was critical of the administration's bill, describing it as "woefully lacking—like using a bean shooter when you should use a gun." He was willing to compromise, however, by substituting the president's bill for legislation he had already introduced, thereby avoiding lengthy new hearings.

Opponents, nevertheless, succeeded in referring the new bill to a subcommittee for a week for more hearings. The hearings were frequently interrupted by quorum calls which Celler angrily denounced as "filibuster by quorum calls."[16] After a month's delay, the committee reported the bill on May 22.

It was then referred to Smith's Rules Committee, where it sat until Bolling forced hearings, over the objection of the chairman. In the middle of the hearings, a quorum was found lacking, and the Rules Committee adjourned for six days.

So it went. Southern Congressmen were able to delay reporting the bill until July 16. Then they tried to rush a debate while liberals were off guard and off the floor. Sensing something in the air, Rayburn knew the time had come for him to act. He found Bolling in the corridor. "You'd better get your boys here quickly," he warned.[17] When Bolling did, the bill passed, 276–126. Less than a week remained, however, before Congress adjourned for the summer and the presidential nominating conventions. The Senate would have little time to act.

Despite the lateness of the session and the opposition of the Senate majority leader, Lyndon Johnson, a few liberals were determined to force a vote before the Senate adjourned. They stationed Senator Paul Douglas of Illinois as a sentry to watch for the bill's arrival from the House on Monday, July 23. His job was to object if the bill was referred to the Senate Judiciary Committee, chaired by James Eastland of Mississippi, where it would be dead for the session.

Douglas watched and waited. Around noon he began to worry. Leaving his station, he walked over to the House side of the Capitol, through the throngs of visitors. In response to his query about the bill, the clerk of the House shuffled through piles of paper. Then a sympathetic congressman told him it had already passed.

Douglas rushed back to the Senate, but he was too late. He had missed the clerk carrying the bill through the labyrinthine hallways, and it had been referred to the Judiciary Committee without objection. There it remained until the Senate adjourned.

In August the issue came up again at the nominating conventions. Presiding for the Democrats, Sam Rayburn became known to millions who were watching on television for the first time. With the lights shining off his bald head, his face grim as he hunched behind the podium, and his voice deep as he pounded the gavel, "Mr. Democrat" was determined not to let civil rights tear the party apart. He and Lyndon Johnson were able to keep any mention of the Supreme Court's controversial desegregation decisions out of the platform. However, a strong minority draft on civil rights was prepared.

When it was time for the convention to decide whether to adopt the platform, Rayburn first called for ayes and noes on the minority draft. After two great roars, he declared that the noes had it. On the majority report, he declared for the ayes. A few state standards waggled for a roll call vote, but Rayburn refused, resting on his parliamentary reputation. "No, no, now just a minute. I have taken the ayes and noes many times, and I think I can tell."[18]

By such inaction in the field of civil rights, Senator Hubert Humphrey warned that Democrats were "digging their own graves."[19] In fact, Democrats lost votes in the cities that year. Black votes swung to the Republicans and to President Eisenhower, who was reelected. Perhaps the time had come to go along.

THE 1957 CIVIL RIGHTS ACT

When Congress convened in 1957, President Eisenhower again asked for a civil rights bill. Once more, the Rules Committee led by Smith tried to prevent a vote on the bill.

Rayburn had been dealing with Smith and the Rules Committee for years. His main tactic in prying bills from the 6–6 tie votes was to work with minority leader Joseph Martin. Offering not only friendship but also patronage, Rayburn would prevail upon Martin to persuade one or two of the more moderate Republicans on the committee to change his vote and break the tie.

Smith, however, had a few tricks, too. He simply refused to call a meeting of the committee. If Rayburn attempted to meet with him, Smith's staff told the Speaker he was not available. Then Smith left town. When he came back, he told reporters that he had gone to his dairy farm in Virginia to inspect a barn that had burned down.

"I knew Howard Smith would do most anything to block a civil rights bill, but I never knew he would resort to arson," Rayburn quipped.[20]

Finally in late spring the Rules Committee reported the 1957 civil rights bill, creating anger among the entire Texas delegation and 100 Southern Democrats. Representative William Colmer of Mississippi, a conservative Democrat on the Rules Committee, said the bill was trying to legislate social values: "You are trying to enforce the love of man for man and you can't do it."[21]

Rayburn, however, was ready to persuade some Southern Democrats to go along. Even though he moved very cautiously on civil rights, he believed the time had come for change. "It's going to be a long pull to reeducate our people to be sure they will do the just and fair thing," Rayburn admitted, but he predicted that in time the South would accept civil rights.[22] He met with backers to plan strategy for passage and lobbied wavering members, especially those from pro-segregation districts. Rayburn persuaded Carl Albert, a representative from a district in Oklahoma just over the border from his Texas district. "Carl, under the Constitution every man has a right to vote," the Speaker said. "You can defend that position before any audience in this country."[23]

Although Chairman Smith made one last effort to kill the bill on a technicality, Rayburn used his parliamentary powers to overrule him. On June 18 the bill passed the House, 286 to 126, with 107 Democrats voting against it.

Again the bill faced stiffer opposition in the Senate. Johnson tried to refer it to the graveyard of the Judiciary Committee, but his point of order failed. Johnson then amended the bill to eliminate one of its strongest provisions. After a filibuster of sixty-six speeches in eight days, the weakened bill passed the Senate. Still it had to go back to the House and the Rules Committee, and Rayburn had to act as a mediator between the two chambers to work out a compromise. A weaker voting rights section was agreed to, and the bill was reported from the Rules Committee and passed.

It was the first civil rights legislation in eighty years, passed by a Democratic Congress and a Republican president. Rayburn felt that the Civil Rights Act of 1957 was a good beginning, "a right to vote bill in its fundamental aspects."[24]

"THE WORST FIGHT OF MY LIFE"

On civil rights, Rayburn found the middle course and supported it with all his personal influence and parliamentary power. That power was still limited, however, by the almost equal power of the Rules Committee. During his last year in the House, the seventy-nine-year-old Speaker confronted Howard Smith one final time.

The confrontation was forced by liberal Democrats who were frustrated at the lack of progressive legislation coming out of a Democratic Congress. Some of them blamed Rayburn for being too old, too out of touch, and too soft on the opposition, but most blamed Southern Democrats who were chairmen of important committees. In 1958 a group of eighty Democrats formed a Democratic Study Group to work for legislation like slum-clearance projects, attacks on crime and disease, lower pollution levels, safer air flights, and improved education. Rayburn promised the DSG that he would persuade the Rules Committee to send all major bills reported out by committees to the floor for votes in 1959 and 1960.

The promise was hard to keep. For one thing, Rayburn's old friend Joseph Martin had been replaced as minority leader in 1959 by Charles Halleck of Indiana. Halleck was less interested in working out compromises with the Democrats. He wanted to create a disciplined Republican opposition to the majority, so he didn't appoint moderates to the Republican positions on the Rules Committee. President Eisenhower, too, seemed less interested in cooperating. He vetoed 181 bills passed in 1959 and 1960. Despite his promise, Rayburn was unable to move the liberal agenda.

Then in 1960 Senator John F. Kennedy won the Democratic nomination for president. The Speaker had backed Lyndon Johnson, but he was won over to the much younger Kennedy and campaigned faithfully for the Democratic ticket. He looked forward to a Democratic Congress and a Democratic president for the first time since Truman.

Kennedy had ambitious plans: for raising the minimum wage, for a Peace Corps, an expanded housing program, medical care for the aged, federal aid to education, and relief for depressed areas. All of Kennedy's hopes rested, however, on whether the Speaker could get around the conservative coalition.

Rayburn had been patient for years, hating to fight fellow Democrats, but he could avoid the confrontation no longer. The issue was clear, he said: "Shall the elected leadership of the House run its affairs, or shall the chairman of one committee run them?"[25]

On New Year's Eve, 1960, Rayburn returned from Bonham, Texas, his family's home now, where he had been mulling over the Rules Committee roadblock. Five Southern Democrats, including William Colmer of Rules, had opposed Kennedy in the election, and House liberals suggested they be stripped of their seniority and choice committee seats. That would take one conservative vote off the Rules Committee. Yet Rayburn hesitated to choose this solution. He didn't like the idea of punishing Democrats after the fact.

The next afternoon, January 1, 1961, he went to the Capitol and called Chairman Smith to his office. In a two-hour conversation, Rayburn told Smith the 6–6 bill-killer votes had to end. He offered a choice: purge Colmer or add three new members to the Rules Committee. The equally aged and savvy Smith said no to both choices.

Two days later, in a maneuver to put pressure on Smith, Rayburn told the press that he favored purging Colmer. Moderate Southerners immediately saw that as a threat to the seniority system. On January 10 they told Rayburn they would support enlargement of the committee instead of the purge.

Still Rayburn mulled over the dilemma. "On tough decisions Mr. Rayburn almost became a loner," said Carl Albert of Oklahoma.[26] The Speaker knew he had enough votes among Democrats to purge Colmer, but he wasn't sure he had enough votes among all House members to expand the committee. If he lost, Smith would be even stronger. Nevertheless, the Speaker chose the more dangerous course: expanding the Rules Committee. The decision made, his shoulders still straight and square, he began what he called "the worst fight of my life."[27]

In his nearly seventeen years as Speaker, Rayburn had done countless favors for representatives: helping them enact pet bills, giving them choice committee assignments, raising campaign funds, and speaking in their home districts. Now he began calling them in. "Are you going with me?" he asked of every possible supporter on the expansion vote.[28]

He knew he could count on few Southern Democrats and that Republican votes would be needed. A week before the scheduled vote, Rayburn didn't have the votes, so he postponed action from January 26 to January 31. Vice President Johnson came down to roam the corridors, buttonholing members to support Rayburn and the president's program. Lobbyists for organizations like the American Medical Association and the Chamber of Commerce talked furiously against the expansion. President Kennedy and his aides joined the fight on Rayburn's side, offering patronage jobs and federal projects to the uncommitted.

On January 31 the galleries were packed once again to witness a power struggle. Not since Norris challenged Cannon had there been such a fierce battle for control of the House. The floor and galleries burst into applause when Rayburn strode up the steps of the rostrum to call the House to order at noon. Only one hour of debate would be allowed.

Chairman Smith spoke against the expansion. He quietly pleaded with the House to postpone action on the bill and promised he wouldn't go home to "milk cows" during the session.[29] Minority Leader Halleck warned that if the floodgates were let down, "we will be overwhelmed with bad legislation."[30]

Speaking last, Rayburn stepped down from the rostrum to the well of the House to make his personal plea. He put the question in plain terms: "We have elected to the Presidency a new leader. He is going to have a program that he thinks will be in the interest of and for the benefit of the American people. I think this House should be allowed on great measures to work its will, and it cannot work its will if the Committee on Rules is so constituted as not to allow the House to pass on those things."[31]

Silence fell during the roll-call vote. At 300 votes, Smith and Rayburn were even. By the end, Rayburn had barely squeaked through, with a vote of 217 to 212. Only 35 of 99 southern Democrats voted for enlargement, but 22 Republicans defected to the Speaker's side. As he left the floor, Rayburn's face was wreathed in smiles. Asked by a reporter how he felt, he responded, "I feel all right. That's about as good as a man can feel. I always feel good when I win."[32]

For a while, Rayburn enjoyed his victory. With the addition of three more members to the Rules Committee,

Kennedy's "New Frontier" legislation eased out of the committee on 8 to 7 votes. An aid-to-depressed-areas bill and an increase in the minimum wage passed Congress. "I'm running the House more nearly now than I ever have before," Mr. Sam told a *Time* reporter.[33]

Rayburn had always devoted himself to his work, investing enormous energy in the job. President Kennedy told the story of a person who had called him at the White House. The caller was told the president was in Canada, the vice president in Southeast Asia, and the secretary of state in Geneva. "Who's keeping the store?" the caller demanded.

"The same man who's alway [sic] kept it—Sam Rayburn!" the operator retorted.[34]

By the summer of 1961, however, Sam Rayburn was in too much pain to be keeping the store. He complained of a backache, and on August 31 went home to Texas, leaving John McCormack as temporary Speaker. His backache was diagnosed as cancer in October, and he died on November 18 in Bonham.

Rayburn was Speaker for sixteen years and 273 days, longer than any other Speaker. During those years he always sought the "sacred center," the way to play a constructive role. "Any jackass can kick a barn down, but it takes a carpenter to build it," he said.[35]

He refused to allow television into the House or into committee hearings. "The normal processes toward good law are not even dramatic, let alone sensational enough to be aired across the land."[36] Good legislating, he thought, is not a quest for glamour but a slow process fraught with pitfalls. Even so, to Rayburn, politics was the ultimate endeavor, "the most honorable profession in the world."[37]

‖6‖

TIP O'NEILL AND THE CONTRAS

"All politics is local."

Thomas P. ("Tip") O'Neill believed in taking care of people. "All politics is local," he liked to say, which meant providing jobs for everyone at decent wages, social welfare programs for those without jobs, and freedom from inflation for all.[1] He especially took good care of the working-class people back home in his Boston district. When his father, Thomas P. O'Neill, Sr., had been a city councilman there, he had handed out snow buttons to unemployed men to exchange for a day's work clearing streets. After young O'Neill was elected to Congress in 1952, he continued to take care of people, coming home every weekend and winning every election he was opposed in by at least 60 percent.

Even in foreign policy, usually the domain of the president, O'Neill brought the issue home to his constituents, both the academics of Harvard and the dockworkers in Charleston. O'Neill had risen quickly in the House under the wing of Majority Leader John McCormack who was also from Massachusetts. Tip's gruff, hearty style, coming from a six-foot-two bulk, endeared him to most congressmen. By 1967, he was a recognized leader, and he loyally defended President Lyndon Johnson and his foreign policy, including the war in Vietnam, because he believed that the domino theory was true: "If we lose in Vietnam, we'll lose in Thailand, Laos, and Cambodia."[2]

One day he was speaking to an audience at Boston College, where his son and daughter were both students, and his information on the war was challenged by a young army officer candidate. In response, O'Neill said he had been briefed forty-three times by high officials in the administration from the president on down.

"That's a lot of briefings," the young man replied, "but how many times have you been briefed by the other side?"[3]

No one had ever asked that question, and the congressman began investigating. He talked to members of the Marine Corps, the Navy, and the CIA and found considerable disagreement and lack of support for the war among the very people charged with fighting it. They did not agree with the domino theory, and they thought the war was unwinnable. Back in Boston on Sunday nights, Tip heard from his own teenage children and their friends how much they opposed the war.

By September 1967, O'Neill had decided continuing the war was wrong. Despite the risk of being thought unpatriotic, he sent a newsletter to the blue-collar workers in his district telling them of his new views. At first only 15 percent of the voters in his district agreed with him, but gradually he began to convince them. He became the most prominent politician opposed to the war and to the foreign policy of a president of his own party. By 1968 Johnson decided not to run for reelection, and American troops were eventually withdrawn under President Richard Nixon.

O'Neill's stand against the war made him acceptable to liberals in the party, and he was a compromise choice for majority whip in 1971. Then, when majority leader Hale Boggs was killed in an airplane crash in 1973, O'Neill stepped into the job. In that position he applied

After serving twenty-four years in the House of Representatives, Tip O'Neill became Speaker in 1976. Here he is shown with his predecessors—on the right, retired Speaker John McCormack, and on the left, Carl Albert, of Oklahoma.

much of the pressure that forced President Nixon to resign because of the Watergate scandal. Tip became Speaker in 1976 as Jimmy Carter was elected president.

A white shock of hair drooping over his forehead, O'Neill dominated the House with his genial personality and 265 pounds. "It helps that Tip is so big," a fellow Democrat said. "He just looks like what you'd think the Speaker of the House should look like."[4] In leadership style he followed the pattern set by Rayburn. He did not engage in crusades but served as the umbrella, putting the right people together to make things work.

O'Neill once told President Carter the story of a father who snipped a map of the world out of a magazine, tore it in pieces, and gave it to his son as a jigsaw puzzle, hoping for a painless geography lesson. The boy swiftly put the map back together. When the surprised father asked how he did it, the boy replied, "Dad, on the back of the map there's a picture of a boy's face. I just put the boy's face together and turned it over, and the map of the world was there."

The point of the story, O'Neill said, "is that if you put the people together rightly, the world will take care of itself."[5]

Putting the right people together, O'Neill managed to push through President Carter's ambitious energy program. Then when Chrysler chairman Lee Iacocca came to him asking for loan guarantees in 1979, O'Neill advised him on the "politics is local" approach. He told Iacocca to find out all the Chrysler employees and dealers in every congressional district and have them write to their representatives about the potential loss of jobs if Chrysler went bankrupt. When that happened, the loan guarantees were approved, with O'Neill's support.

In 1980 Carter ran for reelection but was defeated by Ronald Reagan. As the new President took office, he seemed, on the surface, to have a lot in common with O'Neill. Both were Irish, growing up in relative poverty and working their way through school. Both enjoyed sports and had a gift for storytelling. Both were skilled politicians who preferred to look at the big picture and leave the details to others. Reagan was only two years older.

On issues and friends, however, their paths diverged. Reagan, as governor of California, had become part of what O'Neill snidely called "Beverly Hills Republicans," interested in protecting the wealth of the friends he had gained.[6] Although Tip was friendly with the upper-class Kennedys, his father had made speeches at street-corner rallies to working-class Irish. That was a heritage O'Neill never ignored.

Reagan wanted to cut government spending on domestic matters and confront communism abroad. He knew how to use his popularity and to communicate his conservative beliefs to the public. The public stage was set for a monumental clash between two Irish politicians, between two different views of the world.

In his first term Reagan pushed through a budget that included cuts in social services but large increases for the military. O'Neill thought the budget favored the rich, but he found Congress unable or unwilling to oppose the new president. Reagan's first year in office was the low point of O'Neill's career. When the president's budget came through, the Speaker felt as if he had been hit with a steamroller. "Everything I had fought for, everything I had believed in was being cast aside."[7] He was described that year as bent, burdened, and saddened.[8]

Still, O'Neill would not abandon the politics he loved. "I'm a politician and I'm proud of it," he said.[9] Despite being portrayed by the Republicans as a politician of the old school—old-fashioned and out of touch—O'Neill survived.

When Reagan was reelected in 1984, O'Neill, too, regained his footing and reentered the fray. This term

With Jimmy Carter as president, Speaker Tip O'Neill was able to apply his "politics is local" approach to bring members of the House together and push through Carter's ambitious energy program.

the dominant issue would not be domestic but foreign policy.

In 1979 a revolution led by revolutionaries who called themselves Sandinistas had deposed the dictator Anastasio Debayle Somoza, who had ruled Nicaragua long and brutally with the support of the United States. Although the revolution itself had wide support among the Nicaraguan people, the socialist, Marxist-style government led by the Sandinistas did not. Those disenchanted with the government and former members of Somoza's National Guard joined together loosely to form a group known as the contras. From 1982 to 1988 a civil war raged in Nicaragua, causing 30,000 deaths.

President Carter had remained strictly neutral after the revolution, but to Reagan, Nicaragua represented "one of the greatest moral challenges in post-war history."[10] Reagan believed fiercely in several things, and one was the worldwide Communist threat. He was determined to oppose Communist (or leftist) movements wherever they appeared: Grenada, El Salvador, Cuba, and Nicaragua. If the Sandinistas were not stopped, he warned, they would spread communism throughout Central America; this was the falling-dominoes theory again. In the atmosphere of the cold war between the United States and the Soviet Union and after the "loss" of Vietnam, Reagan was determined to show firm resolve. He vowed to destroy the Sandinistas or at least force them to negotiate with the contras. He was convinced that the contras were "freedom fighters," comparable to the Founding Fathers of the United States rebelling against Great Britain.[11]

As in the Vietnam War, O'Neill heard a different side of the story. His aunt, Sister Eunice, had been a Maryknoll nun in China and elsewhere. Priests and nuns of the Maryknoll order were in Central America as missionaries and health care workers. When they came to the United States on home visits, they stopped by Tip's office. "Their only concern is the welfare of the poor, they don't care about politics," O'Neill said, describing his visitors, and "I haven't met one of them who isn't completely opposed to our policy down there."

To O'Neill, the contras were "racketeers, bandits, and murderers." From the beginning, he had been against aid to the contras. "I've been suspicious of the Reagan administration with respect to Central America ever since they came into office," he said. "I'm not crazy about the Sandinistas, but their country was ravaged by the Somozas and their cronies for forty-five years, when we virtually forced their people into servitude through our corporations. We're not responsible for all of their problems, but we certainly played a part."[12]

O'Neill thought that supporting the contras was the foot in the door for another Vietnam. He was afraid Reagan, after sending money and weapons, would send in the Marines.

"Except as a last resort, the military route is the wrong way to go," he maintained. "If we ever go into Nicaragua, all Americans will come to regret it." Democrats, he vowed, would not allow the United States to become mired in another civil war. As he had with Vietnam, O'Neill would abandon Sam Rayburn's policy, that is, a policy of always supporting the president in foreign policy.

For the first four years of his administration, Reagan had sent money and weapons to the contras without opposition from Congress. The administration merely informed Congress that the Central Intelligence Agency (CIA) was using its contingency fund to supply money, guns, and training. The CIA did not tell Congress, however, that it had also supervised the mining of Nicaragua's harbors, to prevent importation of weapons.[13]

When the mining was revealed in mid-1984, an angry Congress forbade the administration to send any more military aid. In secret, Reagan managed to send supplies

Tip O'Neill and President Ronald Reagan came from similar backgrounds, yet they constantly clashed over appropriations of military aid to the government of El Salvador and the contras in Nicaragua.

first through private groups and then from the sale of arms to Iran. In public, however, the aid had stopped. Whether it should resume was a battle to be fought between the president and the Speaker.

O'NEILL WINS THE FIRST ROUND

In his first major television address after his reelection, Reagan made aid to the contras his top priority. In February 1985 he began a "public education" campaign to gain support. He argued to Congress that foreign policy should be a matter of individual conscience, not an occasion for politicking and arm twisting by the Speaker. A vote against the aid would diminish the office of the presidency in the eyes of the world, he said. When Secretary of State George Shultz testified to a congressional committee, he emphasized stopping communism, but the representatives were skeptical.

By March, House Republican leaders warned Reagan he did not have enough votes for military aid. So on April 3 he sent a request to Congress which he described as a "Central American Peace Proposal." He was asking merely for $14 million of "humanitarian" aid, which would be used only to buy food, clothing, and medicine for the contra armies. The limitations on use of the money would apply for only sixty days, however. If no cease-fire or negotiations had taken place by then, the contras could use the aid for arms and ammunition.

The Speaker of the House responded that the new proposal was a dirty trick, a repackaging of the old military aid package. "I don't think the president of the United States will be happy until troops are in there, and I'm going to do everything in my power to stop that," O'Neill vowed.[14]

The words on both sides became harsher. Reagan portrayed his policy as a test of U.S. resolve to resist communism, so Democrats who opposed it were "soft on communism." As the Sandinistas spread terror north and south, he said, they would "send tens of millions of refugees streaming in a human tidal wave across the border."[15]

In order to stop such rhetoric and shorten the president's lobbying time, O'Neill scheduled a vote on the aid on April 23, a week earlier than expected. When the president called the Speaker an hour before the vote to complain that he was pushing too hard, O'Neill told Reagan his policy was wrong.

After a bitter two-day debate, the House voted against the aid plan, 248 noes to 180 ayes, handing the president one of his most serious defeats.

CONGRESS TURNS AROUND

Just a few days later, Nicaraguan president Daniel Ortega went to Moscow seeking aid, particularly oil. Nicaragua had been suffering under a U.S. boycott imposed by an executive order. Ortega's visit embarrassed those who had voted against contra aid, however, for Reagan had contended that Nicaragua was a Soviet proxy, and Ortega's visit was proving it, he claimed. Sensing a change in congressional mood, Reagan renewed his efforts. This time the House turned around and voted in June to approve $27 million in "nonlethal" aid.

There were some conditions attached. First, the aid would be subject to pledges by Reagan that he was not seeking the overthrow of the Sandinista government. Second, it could not be administered by the CIA or Pentagon. Also, the president would be required to ask for more aid in March of 1986.

What was going on here? Clearly a battle between a Republican executive and a Democratic House but also an unresolved issue. Twenty to thirty swing votes on the issue were affected by what the people back home were saying. The American public seemed confused about what U.S. policy toward Nicaragua really should be.

"Most people don't know where Nicaragua is," GOP leader Robert Michel of Illinois explained,[16] much less what U.S. Central American policy should be. There was no widespread support for Reagan's policy in Nicaragua; despite his lobbying and speeches, the public did not respond with letters and phone calls to their representatives. However, no one really liked the Sandinistas either. Both the country and Congress wavered.

Reagan and O'Neill, however, remained clear in their views. The president never gave up easily on a big issue that he cared about. "He's hardheaded, and he doesn't deviate," O'Neill acknowledged.[17] O'Neill's views, too, had not moderated, and he was equally passionate. The issue seemed to defy his "all politics is local" approach, however. He couldn't find an umbrella big enough or strong enough to hold the Democrats together under the president's persistent challenge.

A SULLIED VICTORY

Six short months after the spring votes, Reagan submitted another request for aid, as required by the 1985 legislation. This time, however, he pulled no punches. He requested $100 million, to come out of Pentagon funds and to include $70 million for military aid. He also wanted to use more money from the CIA and Pentagon contingency funds and to use the aid without any restrictions.

Reagan stepped up his speechmaking. "If we don't want to see the map of Central America covered in a sea of red, eventually lapping at our own borders," he told Jewish leaders, "we must act now."[18] In a television address on March 16, he called the Sandinista government an "outlaw regime." Since the Sandinistas were surrogates for the Soviet Union and Cuba, he said, the Soviets and their allies "will be in a position to threaten the Panama Canal, interdict our vital Caribbean sea lanes, and ultimately move against Mexico."[19]

Democrats accused the president of red-baiting, of labeling anyone who opposed his policy as soft on communism. They thought the threat was less certain. The Sandinistas denied they intended to spread communism. Democrats said the administration should be pushing for negotiations among Central American countries and with the Sandinistas instead of trying to overthrow them. O'Neill warned of escalation: "I see us becoming engaged, step by step, in a military situation that brings our boys directly into the fighting."[20]

On March 20, 1986, the House voted the proposal down, 222 noes and 210 ayes. Reagan called it "a dark day for freedom" and vowed never to give up, "to come back again and again until this battle is over."[21]

O'Neill knew it was not over. He won the March vote partly by his willingness to compromise. He had promised wavering Democrats they would have another chance to vote on a different aid package. So the search for a middle ground began, a way to balance carrot and stick to persuade the Sandinistas to become more democratic.

The compromise that emerged was an alternative developed by Democratic congressman David McCurdy of Oklahoma. It would send only nonmilitary aid to the contras until October 1, 1986. After that, if the president certified that no significant steps were under way to achieve peace in Nicaragua, the House would vote whether to approve $70 million in military aid. O'Neill and the Democratic leadership decided to support McCurdy's plan, which they believed was a compromise that could hold majority support together, that would appeal to a swing group of about forty moderate Republicans and Democrats.

Meanwhile Reagan went to work to oppose any compromise. He made personal telephone calls to representatives he thought might vote either way. He invited them to meetings at the White House and made calls from Air Force One as he flew across the country.

"There is no question in my mind" that the president's lobbying effort is having an effect, O'Neill admitted. He quoted one Democrat who had never before spoken to a president. "I thought I was talking to the pope," the man said and changed his vote. Another Republican, who acknowledged he had trouble naming the countries of Central America, decided to trust Reagan's judgment, in part because he's "a very persuasive fellow."[27]

Thus Reagan's persistence began to wear down the opposition. Representatives were tired of making difficult votes again and again and opposing the president's foreign policy. Nor did they want to appear to be doing nothing. A majority now favored some form of aid to the contras but not military hardware. Reagan insisted that military assistance offered the best hope of convincing the Sandinistas to negotiate seriously. While O'Neill continued to talk to representatives, looking for common ground, Reagan went over his head to the public via television and the media.

Three days before the scheduled vote, a messenger was sent to find O'Neill on the eighth hole of a golf course. The Speaker called an operator at the White House who put him through to Donald Regan, the president's chief of staff. Regan told O'Neill the president wanted to address Congress the next day. O'Neill said, "No problem." He'd schedule a joint session. But the president didn't want that. He wanted to talk only to the House about Central America.

"In other words he wants to lobby," O'Neill said, and refused to allow it. Having the president address one half of Congress on a single issue was unheard of. O'Neill decided Regan was just trying to embarrass him by forcing him to say no; he called it "a cheap political trick."[23] Instead Reagan made a noontime radio and television speech on June 24, the day before the vote.

Both sides predicted the vote for military aid would be close. On June 25 the red lights for no and the green lights for aye flicked on and off during the twenty-minute roll call, most of the time the ayes leading by three or four votes. Members stood in groups watching the lights, occasionally cheering as an undecided voted. George M. O'Brien of Illinois, who was recovering from cancer, appeared in a wheelchair to vote yes. Eleven people changed their votes from the March vote, six Democrats and five Republicans. One hundred million dollars in military aid was passed without any restrictions.

For the first time in six years, the first time in ten separate votes, overt military aid to the contras had been approved. By never compromising, by persisting, by painting Democrats and Tip O'Neill as soft on communism, and without clearly convincing the American people one way or the other, President Reagan had finally won.

Within just a few months, Reagan's victory was sullied. A day after the vote, the International Court of Justice, an arm of the United Nations, said the United States was breaking international law by "training, arming, equipping, financing, and supplying the contra forces."[24]

Then, in the fall of 1986, a contra supply plane was shot down in Nicaragua, and the pilot said he was flying for the CIA. The Reagan administration admitted that weapons had been sold secretly to Iran and part of the profits used to send weapons to the contras. Even as the House had agonized through repeated votes on allowing military aid, that aid was already on its way. The executive branch had acted without the consent of Congress.

At the end of 1986, O'Neill retired, as he had said

Lt. Col. Oliver North is sworn in before a Senate committee investigating the diversion of funds to the Nicaraguan contras from arms sales to Iran. The scandalous covert operation undermined the credibility of the Reagan administration.

When Tip O'Neill retired from the speakership in 1986, Jim Wright of Texas became Speaker. Later, legislation was introduced canceling $40 million in military aid to the contras.

he would. As Jim Wright of Texas became Speaker, legislation was introduced to cancel the last $40 million in aid that had been approved. Under the prodding of President Oscar Arias of Costa Rica, peace negotiations between the contras and the Sandinistas began in December of 1987. With hopes of peace in the air, Congress rejected further aid to the contras in February 1988. In the peace talks, the contras gave up hope of a military victory and the Sandinistas agreed to move toward democracy. Elections in February 1990 resulted in the ousting of the Sandinistas from the government and the election of Violeta Chamorro. A more democratic government emerged after a civil war that caused 30,000 deaths.

Shortly after retiring, O'Neill reflected on the series of votes on contra aid: "Hey . . . we're not in Nicaragua. I played a part in that, and I feel pretty good about it." Five years after the low point of his career, O'Neill went on to claim that "the Reagan revolution is over."[25] His own confrontation with the executive, however, had revealed the weakness of the legislative process, of the "all politics is local" approach, to the even stronger influence of a determined and persuasive president.

EPILOGUE

"SEEKING THE MODERATE MIDDLE"

"Any jackass can kick a barn down. . . ."

Sam Rayburn could have been speaking for O'Neill, Foley, Clay, Reed, and Cannon, too, when he called service the greatest word in the language. For all six, public service was and is a high calling. Speakers believe in the legislative process, in the slow, ponderous decision-making of a democracy, and in politics as a means to a noble end.

They bring different styles to the position—the charm of a Clay, the intellect of a Reed, the persuasiveness of a Rayburn—and they deal with different issues. All successful Speakers, however, must develop a sense of which legislation is important and passable. Most seek the moderate middle, the position the majority of representatives and of the people they represent can support. The Speakers' leadership allows the House to define the issues of the day and to take action on them.

The ability to do this derives not only from the person but from the Speaker's position at the head of a great representative body. The House of Representatives has been described as "the institution of government that most accurately and consistently reflects the sentiments and moods of the American people."[1] If representatives stay in touch with the sentiments and moods of the people, the House shapes legislation that responds to the country's needs.

Nicholas Longworth, a Republican Speaker from 1925 to 1930, called the House "the great dominant, legislative body of the world."[2] Therefore, the Speaker, because he or she is chosen by the members of the House, becomes the "elect of the elected."[3] The Speaker's job is to see that the legislative process resolves conflicts over fundamental social issues, issues that can otherwise divide the nation, as slavery did.

Henry Clay was the first to make the speakership a powerful position. Elected Speaker his first day in the House in 1811, Clay disdained the role of impartial presider and instead used the Speaker's formal powers and the force of his own personality to put the House in order and to prepare for renewed war with Great Britain. Clay's insistence that the Speaker's role was political and he should speak and vote on issues had long-lasting effects. He made the position the second most powerful in the nation.

In 1820 as Speaker and again in 1850 as a senator, Clay was the chief architect of compromises that held the country together and delayed a disastrous civil war. Clay perfected the art of compromise although he was severely criticized for it by advocates on both sides of the slavery issue. In his strenuous efforts to hold the center, he established the model of the Speaker seeking a middle path for the national good.

Although Clay's compromises worked for a time, House unity almost completely broke down in the late 1850s. One hundred and twenty-two ballots were necessary in 1855 to select a Speaker acceptable to both the South and the North. The House spent years recovering from the divisiveness of the period before and after the Civil War. Near the end of the nineteenth century, Thomas Brackett Reed of Maine emerged as a leader who could guide his party and the House toward concerted action.

Reed thought the majority party in Congress, his fellow Republicans, should have the power to govern more decisively, and he made changes in the rules that allowed them to do just that. Where Clay had dominated through the force of his personality, Reed relied on his intellect and sarcastic wit. For Republicans the predominant issues were financial. A protective tariff and sound finance were essential, they thought, to maintaining the nation's bustling economy. Reed brilliantly defended both issues in speeches and became his party's spokesman.

However, the minority was often able to forestall Republican legislation by constantly calling for a quorum. Displaying an iron will, Reed single-handedly changed the rules when he was Speaker in 1890 so that his party could prevail. His rules restored much of the power of the Speaker and of the majority that had dissipated since Clay.

Moving ever so reluctantly into the twentieth century, Joseph G. Cannon continued to use the speakership to push the majority party's program. He employed Reed's Rules from 1903 to 1911 to "stand pat" against the forces of progressivism, the radicals like Theodore Roosevelt, Robert La Follette, and Gifford Pinchot who said the nation must respond to social change. Cannon relied on personal influence, which he developed by constant socializing with his friends, rigid use of the rules, and punishment of those who crossed him.

Uncle Joe finally carried his powers too far, however. The members more sensitive to a need for change in the country couldn't present their views and propose legislation because of his dictatorial reign. He was challenged in a great fight over his control of the Rules Committee in 1910. This successful revolt allowed progressive legislation to be introduced but also reduced the formal powers of the position for succeeding Speakers.

Sam Rayburn found it much more difficult to prevail when he became Speaker in 1940. Rayburn was a persuader, relying on the informal powers of the position and his own reputation for integrity and fairness. When someone compared him to Clay, "the Great Compromiser," Rayburn objected. "I am not a compromiser. I'd rather be known as a persuader. I try to compromise by getting people to think my way."[4]

Serving twice as long as Clay, Rayburn had a decades-long struggle to pry progressive legislation, such as a civil rights bill, out of a Rules Committee dominated by conservatives and Southern Democrats. Through his use of "reasonable persuasion," Rayburn was able to find and lead a majority toward what he came to think was only simple justice. As his last gift to a new president, John F. Kennedy, Rayburn confronted the power of the Rules Committee, expanding its size and appointing members who would report legislation a more liberal majority favored.

Genial Thomas P. ("Tip") O'Neill came up the usual way through the loyal Democratic ranks to become a traditional Speaker, always looking for the umbrella under which to contain a majority. He confronted a popular president, however, who went over the heads of Congress to appeal to the public beyond. In domestic policy the Reagan Revolution prevailed, cutting social welfare spending and increasing the military budget. On the issue of military aid to the contras in Nicaragua, O'Neill fought Reagan passionately, as both sought to avoid the pitfalls of Vietnam, but a persistent president finally prevailed. In foreign policy the House was unable to consistently oppose the will of the executive.

Thomas S. Foley, Speaker since June 1989, continues the tradition of influence through negotiation and persuasion. A moderate Democrat from Washington

State, he has identified the nation's huge debt, growing to almost $4 trillion ($4,000,000,000,000) after years of congressional and executive spending, as the most important issue of the decade. In the fall of 1990 he was hard put to find a majority who would face the potential wrath of their constituents and stand behind deficit-reduction legislation. Yet through persistent prodding of the legislative process, he found that majority.

Foley uses a friendly approach, always looking for consensus. "If you have no sense of what other people's judgments, values or goals are, you're in a very poor position to evaluate how you might accommodate them," Foley says of the negotiating process.[5]

When government was divided—under a Republican president and Democratic Congress—Foley set a tone of nonpartisanship, with the Congress and president working together. Still he remained the leader and definer of his party's position. Like Clay and Rayburn, Foley looks for the middle ground in solving big problems. Speakers who are successful for long periods of time, like Clay and Rayburn, become process people, not issues people.

"Once in a while I've thought, gosh, it'd sort of be fun to go back to being a regular member of a committee and raise hell about something. But there are the responsibilities of trying to bring together opinion and get a result," Foley says.[6] The effective Speaker must be able to moderate his own views, to move toward a national consensus, as Clay did on slavery and Rayburn on civil rights.

Speakers must be constructionists, not destroyers; they must be carpenters and wheel-turners, as Sam Rayburn described them: "Any jackass can kick a barn down, but it takes a carpenter to build it."[7] They must work quietly within the system, or as another Rayburnism expressed it, "The steam that blows a whistle will never turn a wheel."[8]

The Speaker is also the one who slows down legislation, who waits for the majority to form. What are the three best words a legislator can say? According to Rayburn, they were "Wait a minute."[9] Reed and Cannon were especially skeptical of reformers and "reform," which Reed defined as "an indefinable something [that] is to be done, in a way nobody knows how, at a time nobody knows when, that will accomplish nobody knows what."[10]

Can the modern Speaker still be a strong leader? When he became Speaker in 1987, Jim Wright lamented that "If I had been free to choose a time in the last twenty-five years to become Speaker, I wouldn't have chosen this moment. I'm coming to the office at a time when Congress is circumscribed."[11]

Some say the House has become so complex, so diffuse in its leadership, and so subservient to the executive branch that the Speaker will never regain even informal powers such as Rayburn had. The House today has 38 standing committees and 295 subcommittees, each with a chair clamoring for recognition. The House meets for more days of the year and considers more bills than ever before. As a result, representatives have become full-time legislators who stay on their jobs longer. In Foley's Congress, 93 percent of the representatives were reelected. They pay close attention to constituents' views and are often not eager to accept party discipline or leadership.

Moreover, presidents have seized much of the legislative initiative. Since 1933, presidents have submitted a legislative program to Congress, which members of the president's party then push. Even when the majority party in Congress is different from the president's party, that majority finds it difficult to override (with a two-thirds vote) the president's vetoes.

Also, the audience for issues and congressional proceedings has broadened. Members of Congress must be able to sell their ideas. The Speaker must appear on

Speaker Tom Foley and majority leader Richard Gephardt make the traditional courtesy call to the president to notify him that the House has been adjourned.

television commentary shows to build support for his party's views. Trading votes has become less important than influencing public opinion.

Newt Gingrich, the minority leader in the 101st Congress, was chosen not only for his aggressive challenge to the Democrats but because he could use the media. "I'm the first leader of the C-Span [Cable Satellite Public Affairs] generation," he maintains. He uses a confrontational style because, as he puts it, "conflict equals exposure equals power."[12]

In one sense, however, nothing has changed. "The only thing that counts is 218 votes, and nothing else is real," says majority leader Richard Gephardt, Democrat from Missouri.[13] The role of the Speaker is still one of hearing speeches, listening for views, and presiding fairly— but it also means counting votes and seeking a majority. With two political parties, Speaker Reed maintained, "between them both, the world slowly and safely moves ahead. Dreadfully slowly sometimes, but it does always move ahead."[14]

SOURCE NOTES

INTRODUCTION

Observations made on the author's visit to the House of Representatives, March 20, 1991.

CHAPTER ONE

1. Ari Posner, "Friendly Foley," *The New Republic*. August 8, 1988, p. 12–13.
2. *U.S. News & World Report*, June 5, 1989.
3. *Seattle Times*, August17, 1989.
4. Michael Oreskes, "Foley's Law," *The New York Times Magazine*, Nov. 11, 1990, p. 64.
5. *Seattle Times*, August 17, 1989.
6. *Meet the Press*, April 2, 1989.
7. Elizabeth Drew, "Letter from Washington," *The New Yorker*, August 6, 1990, p. 88.
8. Oreskes, *The New York Times Magazine*, p. 68.
9. Ibid.
10. *The New York Times*, October 5, 1990.
11. Schaefer, David. "Foley made emotional plea for budget plan he disliked," *The Seattle Times*, October 5, 1990, A3.

12. "House Votes Stopgap Funds. . . ," *New York Times*, Oct. 6, 1990, p. 1.
13. "Budget crisis deepens by the hour," *Seattle Times*, Oct. 5, 1990, p. A1.
14. *The New York Times*, Oct. 28, 1990.

CHAPTER TWO

1. Booth Mooney, *Mr. Speaker: Four Men Who Shaped the U.S. House of Representatives*. (New Y'ork: Folllett, 1964) p. 22.
2. Mooney, p. 29.
3. Ibid., p. 32.
4. Ibid., p. 30.
5. Ibid., P. 25.
6. Mary P. Follett, *The Speaker of the House of Representatives*. (New York: Longmans, Green, 1896, 1902), p. 73.
7. Glover Moore, *The Missouri Controversy, 1819–1821*. (Lexington, Ky.: University of Kentucky Press, 1966), p. 90.
8. Ibid., p. 91.
9. Ibid., p. 97.
10. Glyndon G. Van Deusen, *The Life of Henry Clay*. (Boston: Little, Brown, & Co., 1937), p. 134.
11. Moore, p. 92.
12. Ibid., p. 339.
13. Van Deusen, p. 143.
14. Ibid., p. 139.
15. Moore, p. 95.
16. Van Deusen, p. 143.
17. Ibid., p. 141.
18. Moore, p. 151.
19. Mooney, p. 46.
20. Ibid., p. 155
21. Ibid., p. 159
22. Ibid., p. 43
23. Thomas Jefferson, Letter of April 22, 1820, in *Thomas*

Jefferson, A Biography in His Own Words. (New York: Newsweek Books, 1974), p. 393.
24. Van Deusen, p. 401.
25. Ibid.
26. Mooney, p. 48.

CHAPTER THREE

1. William Rea Gwinn, *Uncle Joe Cannon, Archfoe of Insurgency.* (New York: Bookman Assoc., 1957), p. 46.
2. Mooney, p. 55.
3. William Alexander Robinson, *Thomas B. Reed, Parliamentarian.* (New York: Dodd, Mead, & Co., 1930), p. 38.
4. *Newsweek*, April 24, 1989, p. 26.
5. Robinson, pp. 106 and 255.
6. Ibid., p. 65
7. Ibid., p. 114.
8. Samuel Walker McCall, *The Life of Thomas Brackett Reed.* (Boston: Houghton Mifflin, 1914), p. 179.
9. Mooney, p. 60.
10. Robinson, p. 167.
11. "Power in Congress," Washington, D.C.: Congressional Quarterly, Inc., 1987, p. 105.
12. Robinson, p. 208.
13. McCall, p. 169.
14. Mooney, p. 62.
15. Robinson, p. 371.
16. Ibid., p. 217.
17. Mooney, p. 56
18. Robinson, p. 268.
19. Ibid, p. 217.
20. Ibid., p. 178.
21. Ibid., p. 178.
22. McCall, p. 196.
23. Robinson, p. 362.
24. McCall, p. 250.

25. Robinson, p. 174.
26. Ibid., p. 125.

CHAPTER FOUR

1. Blair Bolles, *Tyrant from Illinois*. (New York: Norton, 1951), p. 8.
2. Mooney, p. 113.
3. Bolles, p. 5.
4. Ibid., p. 170.
5. Ibid., p. 11.
6. Mooney, p. 125.
7. Bolles, pp. 5, 139.
8. Gwinn, p. 22.
9. Mooney, p. 123
10. Ibid., p. 98.
11. L. White Busbey, *Uncle Joe Cannon: The Story of a Pioneer American*. (New York: H. Holt & Co., 1927), p. 209.
12. Bolles, p. 11.
13. Mooney, p. 98.
14. Ibid., p. 100–1.
15. Booles, p. 151.
16. Gwinn, p. 35.
17. Bolles, p. 216.
18. Gwinn, p. 207–9.
19. Busbey, p. 249.
20. Gwinn, p. 214.
21. Mooney, p. 121.
22. Gwinn, p. 265.
23. Bolles, p. 228.
24. Gwinn, p. 269.

CHAPTER FIVE

1. Mooney, p. 184.
2. Ibid., p. 135.

3. Ibid., p. 137.
4. Ibid., p. 151.
5. *Congress and Its Members*. Third ed. Roger H. Davidson and Walter J. Oleszek. (Washington, D.C.: Congressional Quarterly Press, 1990), p. 161.
6. Mooney, p. 165.
7. C. Dwight Dorough, *Mr. Sam*. (New York: Random House, 1962), p. 399.
8. Alfred Steinberg, *Sam Rayburn, A Biography*. (New York: Hawthorn Books, Inc. 1975), p. 251.
9. Mooney, p. 4.
10. *Congress and the Nation*. Vol. V, 197780, p. 88.
11. William C. Berman, *The Politics of Civil Rights in the Truman Administration*. (Columbus, Ohio, 1970), p. 235.
12. John W. Anderson, *Eisenhower, Brownell and the Congress: The Tangled Origins of the Civil Rights Bill of 1956–57*. (University of Alabama Press, 1964), p. 31.
13. D.B. Hardeman and Donald C. Bacon, *Rayburn: A Biography*. (Austin: Texas Monthly Press, 1987), p. 418.
14. Mooney, p. 129.
15. Ibid., p. 132.
16. Anderson, p. 57.
17. Hardeman, p. 420.
18. Anderson, p. 113.
19. Ibid., p. 126.
20. Steinberg, p. 313.
21. Anderson, p. 69.
22. Steinberg, p. 313
23. Hardeman, p. 421.
24. Dorough, p. 514
25. Hardeman, p. 449.
26. Steinberg, p. 336.
27. Robert L. Peabody and Nelson W. Polsby, *New Perspectives on the House of Representatives*. (Chicago: Rand McNally & Co., 1963), p. 155.

28. Hardeman, p. 457.
29. Steinberg, p. 337.
30. Neil MacNeil, *Forge of Democracy*. (New York: David McKay, 1963).
31. Hardeman, p. 461.
32. Ibid., p. 465.
33. Ibid., p. 467.
34. Steinberg, p. 340.
35. Ibid., p. 350.
36. Mooney, p. 165.
37. Hardeman, p. 429.

CHAPTER SIX

1. Lawrence C. Dodd and Bruce I. Oppenheimer, *Congress Reconsidered*. Third ed. (Washington, D.C.: Congressional Quarterly Press, 1985), p. 261.
2. Tip O'Neill and William Novak, *Man of the House. The Life and Political Memoirs of Speaker Tip O Neill*. (New York: Random House, 1987), p. 190.
3. Ibid., p. 192.
4. Paul Clancy and Shirley Elder, *Tip: A Biography of Thomas O'Neill Speaker of the House*. (New York: Macmillan, 1980), p. 200.
5. Martin Tolchin, "Troubles of Tip O Neill," *New York Times Magazine*, 16 August 1981, p. 43.
6. *The New York Times*, Oct. 7, 1983.
7. O'Neill, p. 345.
8. Tolchin, p. 69.
9. Clancy, p. 227.
10. Stephen Kinzer, *Blood of Brothers, Life and War in Nicaragua*. (New York: G.P. Putnam's Sons, 1991), p. 335.
11. Kinzer, p. 291.
12. O'Neill, p. 369–70.
13. *1985 Congressional Quarterly Almanac*, Washington, D.C.: Congressional Quarterly Press, p. 77.

14. *1986 Congressional Quarterly,* Washington, D.C.: Congressional Quarterly Press, p. 66.
15. Kinzer, p. 291.
16. "Tough Tug of War," *Time,* March 31, 1986, p. 15.
17. "Tip O Neill's Last Hurrah," *Rolling Stone.* December 1986, p. 195.
18. *1986 CQ Almanac,* p. 398.
19. Ibid., p. 399.
20. "Tough Tug of War," p. 15
21. *1986 CQ Almanac,* p. 399.
22. *The New York Times,* June 26, 1986.
23. O'Neill, p. 369.
24. Kinzer, p. 303.
25. "Tip O'Neill's Last Hurrah," p. 165.

EPILOGUE

1. Richard B. Cheney, *Kings of the Hill: Power and Personality in the House of Representatives.* (Continuum, 1983), p. 194.
2. Ibid.
3. *Congress and Its Members,* p. 160.
4. Hardeman, p. 289.
5. *Congress and Its Members,* p. 178.
6. Posner, p. 12.
7. Steinberg, p. 350
8. Ibid., p. 188
9. Ibid.
10. Gwinn, p. 33.
11. *Power in Congress,* p. 2
12. *Congress and Its Members,* p. 175.
13. Ibid., p. 160.
14. McCall, p. 228.

BIBLIOGRAPHY

Bolles, Blair. *Tyrant from Illinois*. New York: Norton, 1951.

Bolling, Richard. *Power in the House*. New York: Dutton, 1968.

Busbey, L. White. *Uncle Joe Cannon: The Story of a Pioneer American*. New York: Henry Holt & Co., 1927.

Champagne, Anthony. *Congressman Sam Rayburn*. New Brunswick, N.J.: Rutgers University Press, 1984.

Cheney, Richard B., and Lynne Cheney. *Kings of the Hill: Power and Personality in the House of Representatives*. New York: Continuum, 1983.

Clancy, Paul, and Shirley Elder. *Tip: A Biography of Thomas O'Neill, Speaker of the House*. New York: Macmillan, 1980.

Davidson, Roger H., and Walter J. Oleszek. *Congress and Its Members*. Third ed. Washington, D.C.: Congressional Quarterly Press, 1990.

Dorough, C. Dwight. *Mr. Sam*. New York: Random House, 1962.

Drew, Elizabeth. "Letter from Washington." *The New Yorker*, August 6, 1990, 88.

Eaton, Clement. *Henry Clay and the Art of American Politics*. Boston: Little, Brown & Co., 1957.

Follett, Mary P. *The Speaker of the House of Representatives*. New York: Longmans, Green, 1896, 1902.

Gwinn, William Rea. *Uncle Joe Cannon, Archfoe of Insurgency.* New York: Bookman Associates, 1957.

Hardeman, D. B., and Donald C. Bacon. *Rayburn: A Biography.* Austin: Texas Monthly Press, 1987.

McCall, Samuel Walker. *The Life of Thomas B. Reed.* Boston: Houghton Mifflin, 1914.

MacNeil, Neil. *Forge of Democracy.* New York: David McKay, 1963.

Mooney, Booth. *Mr. Speaker: Four Men Who Shaped the U.S. House of Representatives.* Chicago: Follett, 1964.

Newhouse, John. "The Navigator," profile of Thomas S. Foley. *The New Yorker.* April 10, 1989, vol. 65, 48.

O'Neill, Tip. *Man of the House: The Life and Memoirs of Speaker Tip O'Neill with William Novak.* New York: Random House, 1987.

Oreskes, Michael. "Foley's Law," *The New York Times Magazine,* Nov. 11, 1990, 64ff.

Posner, Ari. "Friendly Foley," *The New Republic.* August 8, 1988, 12–13.

Robinson, William Alexander. *Thomas B. Reed, Parliamentarian.* New York: Dodd, Mead & Co., 1930.

Steinberg, Alfred. *Sam Rayburn: A Biography.* Alexandria, Va.: Hawthorn Books, Inc., 1975.

"Tip O'Neill's Last Hurrah," *Rolling Stone.* December 18, 1986, 158–60.

Tolchin, Martin. "An Old Pol Takes on the New President," *The New York Times Magazine,* July 24, 1977, 6.

Tolchin, Martin. "Troubles of Tip O'Neill," *The New York Times Magazine.* August 16, 1981, 30–31.

U.S. Capitol Historical Society in cooperation with the National Geographic Society. *We the People: The Story of the U.S. Capitol.* Washington, D.C.: U.S. Capitol Historical Society in cooperation with the National Geographic Society, 1985.

Van Deusen, Glyndon G. *The Life of Henry Clay.* Boston: Little, Brown & Co., 1937.

INDEX

Italicized page numbers indicate illustrations.

Adams, John Quincy, 41, 48
Agriculture Committee, 85
Albert, Carl, 113, 116, *121*
American Federation of Labor, 82
American System, 38
Appropriations Committee, 77
Arias, Oscar, 136

Bailey, Joseph Weldon, 94
Ballinger, Richard A., 87
Bankhead, William B., 92, 99
Benson, Thomas Hart, 48
Bentsen, Lloyd, 25
Boggs, Hale, 120
Bolling, Richard, 108, 110, 111
Brady, Nicholas, 25
Brownell, Herbert, 107
Brown v. *Board of Education*, 107, *109*

Bryan, William Jennings, 70
Budget process, 24
Bush, George, 23, 25, 27, 30

Calendar Wednesday rule, 84, 87
Calhoun, John C., 51
Cannon, Joseph G., 18, 65, 72, *78*, 139–40, 142
  background of, 74
  electoral defeat, 90
  final years, 92
  "hayseed" reputation, 76–77
  leadership style, 73–74, 77, 79, 82–83
  reforms, opposition to, 75, 79, 80, 82
  revolt against, 83–84, 85, 87–90
  tariffs and, 84–85
Carter, Jimmy, 122, *124*, 125
Celler, Emanuel, 110
Central Intelligence Agency (CIA), 126

155

INDEX

Chamorro, Violeta, 136
Chase, Salmon, 52
Chrysler bailout, 122
Civil rights, 101–2
    Civil Rights Act of 1957, 112–14
    Civil Rights Bill of 1956, 107–8, 110–11
    poll tax, 102, 103
    school desegregation, 107
    southern opposition, 108
    Truman's initiative, 102–3, 105
    voting rights, 108
Clark, Champ, 65, 84, 90
Clay, Henry, 17, 32–33, *49*, 55, 138
    committees and, 35
    Compromise of 1850, 48, 51–52, 54
    conciliatory style, 46, 48
    early years, 33
    as Great Compromiser, 38
    Missouri Compromise, 39–44, 45–48
    personality of, 34
    rules, enforcement of, 35–36
    slave ownership, 33, 41–42
    speaking skills, 36, 42–43
    War of 1812, 33–35, 36
Cleveland, Grover, 66, 68
Cobb, Thomas, 41
Colmer, William, 113, 115, 116

Committee of the Whole, 35
Committee system, 35, 83
Compromise of 1850, 48, 51–52, 54
Consensus, 10, 11, 17
Conservation movement, 80, 85, 87
Constitution, 61, 88, 107
    slavery and, 39
Contras, 125–26, 128–33, 136

Dalzell, John, 87
Darman, Richard, 25, 30
Debate procedures, 35–36
Deficit problem
    causes of, 19–20
    difficulty of dealing with, 24–25
    growth of deficit, 19, 25
    House action on, 27, 28–31
    reduction plans, 25, 27, 30
Democratic conventions
    1948, 103
    1956, 111–12
Democrats, 64
Dewey, Thomas, 103
Divided government, 23
Dixiecrats, 103, 104
Domino theory, 120, 125
Douglas, Paul, 111
Douglas, Stephen, 52, 54

Eastland, James, 111
Edwards, Mickey, 23–24
Eisenhower, Dwight D., 107, 112, 115

156

INDEX

Fair Employment Practices Commission, 101
Filibusters, 59, 60, 89
Fillmore, Millard, 54
Foley, Heather, 21
Foley, Thomas, 18, *22*, *26*, 140–41, *143*
  career of, 21
  conciliatory style, 21, 23–24, 27–28
  deficit problem, 19, 24–25, 27, 28–31
  views on Congress and speakership, 9–15
Follett, Mary, 36
Forrest, Thomas, 43

Garner, John Nance, 96, 97
Gephardt, Richard, 19, 25, 27, 28–29, *143*, 144
Gingrich, Newt, 144
Gompers, Samuel, 80, *81*, 82
Gramm-Rudman-Hollings law, 24, 25
Gray, William, 27
Great Depression, 97, *98*

Halleck, Charles, 115, 117
Harrison, Benjamin, 67
Hayes, George, *109*
Henderson, George, 77
House of Representatives, 10, 16–17
  complexity of proceedings, 142, 144
  disorderliness of, 58
  early history, 32
  power sharing, 23
  procedural reforms, 59–62, 64, 71
  as reflection of American people, 137–38
  See also Speakership; *specific committees*
Humphrey, Hubert, 103, 112

Iacocca, Lee, 122
International Court of Justice, 133
Interstate and Foreign Commerce Committee, 96, 97
Interstate Commerce Commission (ICC), 80
Iran-contra scandal, 133, *134*

Jackson, Andrew, 36
Jefferson, Thomas, 10–11, 48
Johnson, Lyndon B., 111, 112, 113–14, 115, 116, 119, 120
Judiciary Committee, 85, 110

Keifer, J. Warren, 58
Kennedy, John F., 115, 117, 118, 140
Kilgore, C. Buckley, 62, 64

Labor movement, 80, 82
La Follette, Robert, 75, 80, 83, 139
Lesinski, John, 105
Lodge, Henry Cabot, 71
Longworth, Nicholas, 138

McCormack, John, 118, 119, *121*

INDEX

McCurdy, David, 131
McKinley, William, 70, 71
Madison, James, 11, 34
Majority rule issue, 64, 71–72
Marshall, Thurgood, *109*
Martin, Joseph, 112, 114
Mexican-American War, *50*, 51
Michel, Robert, 130
Missouri Compromise
    admission as state, 38–44
    constitutional issue, 44–48
Monroe, James, 44, 45
Muhlenberg, Frederick, 32

Nabrit, James, Jr., *109*
New Deal, 97, 99
New Frontier, 118
Nicaragua, 125–26, 129, 136. *See also* Contras
Nixon, Richard, 120, 122
Norris, George W., 73–74, 76, 79–80, 83, 85, 87, 88, 89–90
North, Col. Oliver, *134*

O'Brien, George M., 133
O'Neill, Thomas P., Sr., 119
O'Neill, Thomas P. ("Tip"), 18, 21, 27, *121*, *124*, *127*, 140
    contras and, 125–26, 128, 129, 130, 131, 132–33
    leadership style, 122
    local orientation, 119
    as majority leader, 120, 122
    personality of, 122
    Reagan and, 122–23
    retirement from Congress, 133, 136
    Vietnam War, 119–20
Ortega, Daniel, 129

Pinchot, Gifford, 85, *86*, 87, 139
Poll tax, 102, 103
Presidential elections
    1820, 44–45
    1948, 103
Progressive movement, 74–76, 79–80, 82, 90, 92
Public service, 137

Quorums issue, 57, 60–62, 64, 68

Railroads, 74–75, 80
Randolph, John, 35, 36, 41, 43–44, 46
Rayburn, Sam, 18, 57, *95*, 126, 137, 140, 141, 142
    civil rights, personal feelings about, 102, 113
    Civil Rights Act of 1957, 112–14
    Civil Rights Bill of 1956, 107, 111
    committee chairmanship, 97, 99
    Democratic conventions, 103, 111–12
    early years, 93–94

INDEX

election to Congress, 93, 94
issues of interest to, 96
leadership style, 105
personality of, 97
Rules Committee and, 104–5, 114–18
school desegregation, 107
sensitivity to Representatives' moods, 108, 110
speakership, elevation to, 99
Truman's civil rights initiative, 102–3, 105
voting rights, 108
World War II draft, 99, 101

Reagan, Ronald, *127*
budget of, 123
contra policy, 125, 126, 128–33
deficit problem, 20
Iran-contra scandal, 133
O'Neill and, 122–23

Reed, Thomas Brackett, 17, 57, 59, 60, *63*, 77, 92, 138–39, 142, 144
economic views, 65
humor of, 62
legislative style, 65
majority rule issue, 64, 71–72
personality of, 58
quorums issue, 57, 60–62, 64, 68
"Reed's Rules," 62
sound finance, 65, 68, 69–70

Spanish-American War, 70–71
tariffs, 65–69, 70

Regan, Donald, 132
Republicans, 64, 76
Roosevelt, Franklin D., 97, 101
Roosevelt, Theodore, 80, 85, 90, 92, 139
Rules Committee, 13, 59, 62, 67, 77, 82, 84, 112
civil rights legislation and, 108, 110–11, 112–13, 114
expansion of (1961), 114–18
Norris reforms, 88–90
twenty-one-day rule, 104–5
Rural Electrification Administration Act of 1936, 99

Sandinistas, 125, 126, 129, 130–31, 136
School desegregation, 107
Securities Act of 1933, 97
Senate, civil rights legislation and, 111, 113–14
Seniority system, 12–13, 116
Seward, William, 52
Shultz, George, 128
Sinclair, Upton, 80
Slavery, 33
Compromise of 1850, 48, 51–52, 54
Constitution and, 39
disunion issue and, 41, 48, 51

INDEX

Slavery *(cont.)*
   Missouri Compromise, 38–48
   North-South disagreement over, 38
Smith, Howard W., 108, 110, 112–13, 114, 116, 117
Smith, Walter I., 87
Somoza Debayle, Anastasio, 125
Sound finance, 65, 68, 69–70
Southern Manifesto, 108
Spanish-American War, 70–71, 77
Speakership, 9, 10, 12
   chair of Speaker, 16
   early history, 32
   moderate middle, search for, 137
   most important task, 11
   powers of, 13
   strong leadership in 1990s, 142, 144
Sununu, John, 25, 30
Supreme Court, 107

Taft, William H., 83, 84, 85, 87, 90

Tallmadge, James, 40, 41
Tariffs, 65–69, 70, 84–85, 96
Taylor, John W., 43
Taylor, Zachary, 51, *53*, 54
Thomas, Jesse B., 42
Thurmond, Strom, 103
Truman, Harry, 101–2, 103, *106*

Utility Holding Company Act, 99

Vietnam War, 119–20
Voting rights, 108

War of 1812, 33–35, 36, *37*
Ways and Means Committee, 96
Webster, Daniel, 51
White, William Allen, 57
Wilson, Woodrow, 90, *91*, 93, 96
World War II draft, 99, *100*, 101
Wright, Jim, 21, *135*, 136, 142